# INSTANT REFERENCE

# GEOGRAPHY

TEACH YOURSELF®

For UK orders: please contact Bookpoint Ltd, 78 Milton Park, Abingdon, Oxon OX14 4TD. Telephone: (44) 01235 400414, Fax: (44) 01235 400454. Lines are open 9.00-6.00, Monday to Saturday, with a 24-hour message answering service. E-mail address: orders@bookpoint.co.uk

For USA and Canada orders: please contact NTC/Contemporary Publishing, 4255 West Touhy Avenue, Lincolnwood, Illinois 60646-1975, USA. Telephone: (847) 679 5500, Fax: (847) 679 2494.

Long renowned as the authoritative source for self-guided learning — with more than 40 million copies sold worldwide — the *Teach Yourself* series includes over 200 titles in the fields of languages, crafts, hobbies, business, computing and education.

*British Library Cataloguing in Publication Data*
A catalogue record for this title is available from the British Library.

*Library of Congress Catalog Card Number:* On file

First published in UK 2000 by Hodder Headline Plc, 338 Euston Road, London NW1 3BH.

First published in US by NTC/Contemporary Publishing, 4255 West Touhy Avenue, Lincolnwood (Chicago), Illinois 60646-1975, USA.

The 'Teach Yourself' name and logo are registered trademarks of Hodder & Stoughton.

Text Consultant: Dr Joanna Bullard, Loughborough University
Text Editor: Elizabeth Martyn
Typeset by TechType, Abingdon, Oxon
Printed in Great Britain for Hodder & Stoughton Educational, a division of Hodder Headline Plc, 338 Euston Road, London NW1 3BH, by Cox & Wyman Ltd, Reading, Berkshire.

Impression number    10 9 8 7 6 5 4 3 2 1
Year                 2006  2005  2004  2003  2002  2001  2000

# Contents

Bold type in the text indicates a cross reference. A plural, or possessive, is given as the cross reference, i.e. is in bold type, even if the entry to which it refers is singular.

## abiotic factor

A factor such as temperature, light or soil structure, which is not of animal or plant origin and which affects the life of organisms within an **ecosystem**. Sulphur dioxide emissions from a power station are an example of a harmful abiotic factor, because they produce **acid rain** which is damaging to plants and people.

## ablation

The loss of snow or ice from a **glacier** by melting and evaporation.

- Ablation takes place near the snout, or foot, of a glacier, because temperatures are higher at lower altitudes.
- If ablation is greater than the accumulation of new snow and ice, the glacier will retreat.
- Ablation is fastest during summer, when it is warm.

## abrasion

When rock fragments carried by rivers, wind, ice or the sea scrape and grind away a surface, they cause abrasion. It is common to see ridges or grooves on rocks, and these are abrasions caused when the surfaces were scratched by frozen debris in a glacier. This kind of **erosion** is called **corrasion**.

**See also**: *coastal erosion*.

## abyssal plain

The broad expanse of sea floor lying 3–6 km/2–4 mi below sea level. Abyssal plains are found in all the major oceans, and they extend from bordering continental rises to the ocean ridges.

Abyssal plains are underlain by outward-spreading, new oceanic **crust** extruded from ocean ridges and are covered in deep-sea sediments derived from continental slopes and floating microscopic marine organisms. The plains are interrupted by chains of volcanic islands and **seamounts**.

Otherwise, the abyssal plains are very flat, with a slope of less than 1:1000.

The dark ocean region above the abyssal plain 2,000–6,000 m/ 6,500–19,500 ft deep is called the abyssal zone. Three-quarters of the area of the deep-ocean floor lies in the abyssal zone, which has a temperature 4°C/39°F and is too far from the surface for photosynthesis to take place. Some fish and crustaceans living there are blind or have their own light sources.

## acid rain

When acidic gases like sulphur dioxide and oxides of nitrogen are released into the atmosphere, they dissolve in pure rainwater to make acid rain. These gases come from factories, power stations where coal is burned, and car exhaust fumes.

Acidity is measured on the **pH scale**, where the value of 0 represents liquids and solids that are completely acidic and 14 represents those that are highly alkaline. Distilled water is neutral and has a pH of 7. Normal rain, with a pH value of 5.6, is slightly acidic due to the presence of carbonic acid formed by the mixture of carbon dioxide and rainwater. Acid rain has values of 5.6 or less on the pH scale.

Acid rain damages buildings, and alters the chemical balance of soil. Plants and trees growing in this soil become prone to disease and may die. Minerals from the soil are washed into lakes and rivers where they damage fish and kill plankton. Forests and lakes have been harmed by acid rain in Scandinavia, Europe, and eastern North America.

Acidic gases can travel over 500 km/310 mi per day. Acidic **deposition** comes not just from mist, rain, or snow, but can also fall from the atmosphere as dry particles. Water, plants, and masonry can also absorb acids directly from the gases themselves.

---

### REDUCING EMISSIONS OF ACIDIC GASES

During the last 20 years, emissions of sulphur dioxide have fallen by over half. There is still more to do, by:

- fitting more efficient burners in power stations
- using gas instead of coal in power stations
- fitting catalytic converters to all new road vehicles.

## aerial photography
Photographs taken from high levels by cameras fixed in aircraft or satellites, show up surface features that cannot be seen from the ground. These are particularly useful to geologists, surveyors, engineers, and meteorologists. Archaeologists use them to work out where buildings used to stand, since crops seen from above have a different colour if they are growing over the buried foundation of a wall.

## afforestation
The planting of large numbers of trees on land where none have been grown before. The trees are used:
- to provide timber and wood pulp
- for firewood
- to bind soil together and prevent **erosion**
- to act as windbreaks.

Afforestation is controversial, because new plantations usually consist of conifers. These trees acidify the soil, and do not sustain wildlife. Many ancient mixed woodlands are being lost, and replacing them with conifers conflicts with the aims of **biodiversity** because the conifers are not as eco-logically valuable as the trees they are replacing.
   **See also**: *deforestation*.

## Africa
Second largest of the continents, and also the hottest, Africa is divided into 54 countries, with a total population of 750 million, which is estimated to have risen to 900 million by 2000. Africa is connected to Asia by the

---

**AFRICAN INDUSTRIES**

- minerals, including diamonds, gold, and crude petroleum
- cocoa
- coffee
- groundnuts
- hardwood timber
- tourism is important in East Africa, where visitors come to see the animals of the savannah grasslands.

isthmus of Suez, and separated from Europe by the Mediterranean Sea. Almost all of Africa lies within the **Tropics**, so the climate is hot all year round, with definite wet and dry seasons. Drought is a constant problem, and 25 million people living in sub-Saharan Africa are facing famine.

There are three mountain systems in Africa. In the north, the Atlas mountains separate the coastal countries from the Sahara desert. Mountains also flank the west and east coasts. The eastern range contains Kilimanjaro, the highest African peak, at 5,900m/19,364 ft.

For its size, Africa has few rivers and many are not navigable, because of long stretches of cataracts. The most important rivers are the Nile, Congo-Zaire, Zambezi, and Niger. The coastline of Africa is regular and relatively short, considering the size of the country, because it has no deep bays or estuaries. There are few islands off the African coast, and most are small, apart from Madagascar, which has a population of 10 million.

Africa is home to a uniquely diverse range of animals. The Sahara desert to the north of the country formed a barrier which kept predators out, and

---

**FACTS ABOUT THE AFRICAN CONTINENT**

- The total area of Africa is 30,097,000 sq km/11,620,451 sq mi, three times the area of Europe.
- The African continent is dominated by a uniform central plateau comprising a southern tableland with a mean altitude of 1,070 m/3,000 ft that falls northwards to a lower elevated plain with a mean altitude of 400 m/1,300 ft. There are no great alpine regions or extensive coastal plains.
- The highest points are Mount Kilimanjaro at 5,900 m/19,364 ft and Mount Kenya at 5,200 m/17,058 ft.
- The lowest point is Lac Assal in Djibouti at −144 m/−471 ft below sea level.
- The Sahel is a narrow belt of savanna and scrub forest which covers 700 million hectares/1.7 billion acres of west and central Africa.
- The Great Rift Valley in the east is an area in which the continent is rifting apart. This **rift valley** contains most of the great lakes of East Africa (except Lake Victoria).
- Africa's Sahara Desert is the world's largest desert in the north. Other deserts include the Namib, Kalahari, and Great Karoo in the south.

allowed many species to flourish undisturbed. The most spectacular animals are found in the open **savannah** that occupy much of Africa south of the Sahara. Herbivorous species include elephants, zebra, wildebeest, gazelle, giraffe, and rhinoceros. A variety of carnivorous animals, such as the cheetah, lion, leopard, and jackal, prey on these creatures. Besides large animals, Africa boasts an exceptionally wide variety of birds, including parrots and flamingos; reptiles, such as crocodiles, pythons, and lizards; fish; and insects.

*African wetlands*
The extensive African wetlands range from the vast swamps of the upper Nile drainage system to the huge lakes which are so notable a feature of the Rift Valley. They are of unusual biological diversity and richness, as exemplified by Africa's 2,000 species of freshwater fishes, compared with Europe's 50. They range from the primitive lungfish to the Nile perch, which can reach a weight of more than 130 kg.

These extensive wetlands serve as natural reservoirs; they collect water during the rainy season and hold it during the dry. As the dry season advances, herds of grass-eaters, driven from the savannas by lack of pasturage and water, fall back on the wetlands. Springbok, gemsbok, and eland, for example, migrate from the Kalahari Desert into the wetlands of the Okovango Delta. There they join the more permanent residents of the flood-plain, such as the waterbuck, as well as such typical woodland species as kudu, roan, and sable antelope, among others. These dry-season flood plain concentrations are exceptionally impressive.

**See also**: *rainforest.*

## Agenda 21
A non-binding treaty, signed by representatives of 178 countries in 1992, which sets out a framework of recommendations designed to protect the environment and achieve sustainable development. The treaty highlights the importance of international cooperation, but also discusses the role of individuals, communities, and local authorities in attaining the goals it sets out.

## agribusiness
Farms run commercially as industries. Agribusiness farms are very large, highly structured, and fully mechanized. These farms are dependent on chemicals, and are often financed by multinational corporations, whose main interests lie outside agriculture.

## agricultural revolution

Sweeping changes that took place in Europe in the 18th century to make agriculture more productive by using scientific farming methods. This was in response to rapidly rising populations which meant that a growing demand for food had to be met. Mechanization made considerable progress in the USA and Europe in the 19th century and also dramatically increased agricultural productivity.

**See also**: *crop rotation.*

---

### MAJOR EVENTS OF THE AGRICULTURAL REVOLUTION

**Development of improved breeds of livestock**. In Britain, Robert Bakewell (1725-1795) improved the quality of cattle and sheep by using inbreeding.

**Introduction of four-course crop rotation**. English agriculturalist Jethro Tull (1674-1741) invented this system for rotating crops so that different nutrients would be absorbed from the soil at different times.

**Use of new crops such as potatoes, red clover and turnips for winter animal fodder**. This did away with the need to slaughter animals in autumn and made fresh meat available all year round.

**Invention of agricultural machinery**. The seed drill had been invented in 1701. Later, new machines such as a thresher, plough and harvester arrived in Europe from the USA.

---

## agriculture

All types of farming, including cultivating the soil to grow **crops**, and raising **livestock**. Farms can be owned by individuals, corporations, or entire communities. The last 50 years have seen a huge growth in the use of chemicals such as weedkillers and **fertilizers** in farming. Intensive farming of cattle, poultry, and pigs is common in industrialized countries. There has also been a reaction against some forms of agriculture, because of **pollution** of the **environment** and suffering caused to animals. Alternative methods, such as **organic farming**, have sprung up in response to this.

**See also**: *agrochemical, arable farming, cooperative farming, dairy farming, European Union, pastoral agriculture, smallholding.*

## agrochemical
Artificially produced chemical used in intensive farming. Agrochemicals include nitrate and phosphate **fertilizers**, pesticides, some animal-feed additives, and pharmaceuticals. Many of these cause **pollution** and almost all are avoided by **organic** farmers.

## agroforrestry
Any agricultural system that involves planting and maintaining trees on land where crops and animals are also raised. The trees may be used for timber, fuel, food, or animal fodder. Trees may be interplanted with other crops in order to provide shade, reduce soil erosion, and increase moisture retention in the soil. Leaves dropped by the trees also improve the fertility of the soil.

## aid, development
Money given or loaned by industrialized countries to developing nations. Each country spends more than half its contribution on giving help directly to countries with which it has historical or military links, or with whom it would like to trade. The balance goes to international organizations, such as the United Nations and World Bank, for distribution. Although all industrialized members of the United Nations are committed to giving at least 0.7% of their **gross national product** to aid, the UK and the USA have not achieved this target.

## air pollution
Contamination of the atmosphere by a wide range of toxic substances discharged into the air by factories and car exhausts. The main air pollutants are sulphur dioxide and oxides of nitrogen, which are responsible for the damage caused by **acid rain**.

## Major air pollutants

| Pollutant | Sources | Effects |
|---|---|---|
| Sulphur dioxide ($SO_2$) | oil, coal combustion in power stations | acid rain formed, which damages plants, trees, buildings, and lakes |
| Oxides of nitrogen ($NO$, $NO_2$) | high-temperature combustion in cars, and to some extent power stations | acid rain formed |
| Lead compounds | from leaded petrol used by cars | nerve poison |
| Carbon dioxide ($CO_2$) | oil, coal, petrol, diesel combustion | greenhouse effect |

## Major air pollutants (*continued*)

| Pollutant | Sources | Effects |
|---|---|---|
| Carbon monoxide (CO) | limited combustion of oil, coal, petrol, diesel fuels | poisonous, leads to photochemical smog in some areas |
| Nuclear waste | nuclear power plants, nuclear weapon testing, war | radioactivity, contamination of locality, cancers, mutations, death |

Air pollution from leaded petrol has been shown to cause learning impairment in children living near major roads. Europe is committed to reducing harmful gas emissions by 8% by 2012.

## Air pollution in the world's megacities

| Rank | City* | Total suspended particulates** (micrograms per cubic metre) |
|---|---|---|
| 1 | Delhi | 415 |
| 2 | Beijing | 377 |
| 3 | Calcutta | 375 |
| 4 | Mexico City | 279 |
| 5 | Jakarta | 271 |
| 6 | Shanghai | 246 |
| 7 | Bombay | 240 |
| 8 | Bangkok | 223 |
| 9 | Manila | 200 |
| 10 | Rio de Janeiro | 139 |

*Urban areas with more than 10 million people by the year 2000, for which reliable data is available.
**Total suspended particulates refer to smoke, soot, dust, and liquid droplets from combustion that are in the air. They indicate the quality of the air a population is breathing

*Source: World Development Indicators 1998, IBRD/World Bank, 1998*

## albedo
The amount of light reflected by a particular surface. A white or light-coloured surface reflects more light than a dark one. On average, the **Earth's** surface has an albedo of 30%. On snowy areas, this figure could become as high as 95%, while on dark soil it could be as low as 10%.

## alluvial fan
When a river or stream flowing down a slope enters a plain, it slows down and deposits its load of alluvium. This sediment forms a roughly triangular

**EXAMPLES OF AIR POLLUTION**

■ Possibly the world's worst ever human-made air pollution disaster happened in Indonesia in September 1997. Smoke pollution from forest clearance fires reached 7.5 mg per cu m in the city of Palangkaraya (nearly 3 mg more than in the London smog of 1952 in which 4,000 people died). The pollutants spread to Malaysia and other countries of the region.

■ The greatest single cause of air pollution in most developed countires is the car, which is responsible for 85% of the carbon monoxide and 45% of the oxides of nitrogen present in the atmosphere.

■ A 1997 survey of contamination in mosses taken from different countries showed that Slovakia and southern Poland are the most polluted areas in central Europe, with high levels of heavy metal pollutants, including cadmium, lead, copper, and zinc, caused by chemical and metal smelting industries in Slovakia, the northeastern Czech Republic, and Poland.

shape called an alluvial fan at the base of the slope. Its surface slopes outward in a wide arc, but in time the fan is destroyed by erosion.

**See also**: *alluvium*.

**alluvium**
Fine gravel and silt deposited by a **river**. Alluvium is dropped along the river channel where the water's speed is too low to carry the river's load, for example, on the inside bend of a **meander**. A **flood plain** is made of alluvium dropped by floodwater which can also result in **oxbow lakes**. A deposit at the mouth of a river entering the sea is known as marine alluvium.

**See also**: *alluvial fan*.

**Antarctica**
Antarctica is the coldest of all continents and surrounds the **South Pole**. The whole region, including the seas, is described as the Antarctic. Antarctica occupies 10% of the world's surface, and contains 90% of the world's ice, representing nearly three-quarters of its fresh water. It is thought that if all the ice suddenly melted, the world sea level would rise by 60 m/197 ft.

Antarctica is divided into two regions, separated by the Transantarctic Mountains. Two vast seas, the Ross Sea and the Weddell Sea, cut into the continent. Between them lies the mountainous Antarctic Peninsula, which was originally connected to **South America** millions of years ago. Mount Erebus on Ross Island is the world's southernmost active **volcano**.

Only around 2% of the land is ice-free. The snow in the Antarctic rarely melts but accumulates into massive ice caps with an average thickness of approximately 2,000 m/6,600 ft. As the ice caps grow, the weight of the ice squeezes the ice cap sideways towards the coast, where ice shelves extend out into the surrounding seas. These fringing ice shelves are broken up by ocean tides and waves, creating icebergs.

The combination of cold air, high winds, and blowing snow makes Antarctica's climate the severest in the world. The average annual temperature at the South Pole is –49°C/–56°F. **Precipitation** is largely in the form of snow or hoar-frost rather than rain, which rarely exceeds 50 mm/2 in per year (less than the Sahara Desert). The Antarctic ecosystem is characterized by large numbers of relatively few species. Only two species of flowering plant are known in the Antarctic. There are five animal species which breed ashore during the winter months: emperor penguins, king penguins, wandering albatross, grey petrel, and the grey-winged petrel. Cod, icefish, and krill are fished in Antarctic waters. Petroleum, coal, and minerals such as palladium and platinum exist, but their exploitation is prevented by a 50-year ban on commercial mining. No people live here permanently and settlement is limited to scientific research stations with a maximum population of 10,000 during the summer months.

## Chronology of Antarctic exploration

**1773–74**  English explorer James Cook first sails in Antarctic seas, but exploration is difficult before the development of iron ships able to withstand ice pressure.

**1819–21**  Antarctica is circumnavigated by Russian explorer Fabian Bellingshausen.

**1823**  Belgian-born British navigator James Weddell sails into the sea now named after him.

**1841–42**  Scottish explorer James Ross sights the Great Ice Barrier now named after him.

**1895**  Norwegian explorer Carsten Borchgrevink is one of the first landing party on the continent.

**1898**  Borchgrevink's British expedition first winters in Antarctica.

**1901–04**  English explorer Robert Scott first penetrates the interior of the continent.

**1907–08**  English explorer Ernest Shackleton comes within 182 km/113 mi of the Pole.

**1911**  Norwegian explorer Roald Amundsen reaches the Pole, 14 December, overland with dogs.

**1912**      Scott reaches the Pole, 18 January, initially aided by ponies.

**1928–29**   US naval officer Richard Byrd makes the first flight to the Pole.

**1935**      US explorer Lincoln Ellsworth first flies across Antarctica.

**1946–48**   US explorer Finn Ronne's expedition proves the Antarctic to be one continent.

**1957–58**   International Geophysical Year, involving 12 countries setting up research stations; this leads to the 1959 Antarctic Treaty. English explorer Vivian Fuchs makes the first overland crossing.

**1959**      A Soviet expedition crosses from the West Ice Shelf to the Pole. The International Antarctic Treaty is signed by 39 countries, and suspends all territorial claims, reserving an area south of 60° south latitude for peaceful and scientific purposes only.

**1961–62**   The Bentley Trench is discovered, which suggests that there may be an Atlantic–Pacific link beneath the continent.

**1966–67**   Specially protected areas are established internationally for animals and plants.

**1985**      A hole in the ozone layer over Antarctica is discovered by the British Antarctic Survey.

**1991**      The Antarctic Treaty imposing a 50-year ban on mineral exploitation is secured, signed by the 39 signatories of the 1959 treaty.

**1992**      US geologists find evidence of active volcanoes beneath the ice.

**1995**      The disintegration of the Prince Gustav Ice Shelf and the northern Larsen Ice Shelf – as a result of global warming – is discovered.

**1996**      A 14,000 sq km/5,400 sq mi freshwater lake is discovered beneath the Antarctic ice. It is estimated to be 5 million years old.

## anticyclone

As air descends it becomes warm and dry and creates an area of high atmospheric pressure called an anticyclone.

- Anticyclones are characterized by clear weather.
- They do not bring rain or strong winds.
- In summer anticyclones bring hot, sunny days and in winter fine, frosty spells.
- In some countries anticyclones can cause fog and low cloud.
- Blocking anticyclones can cause summer droughts and severe winters.

## aquifer

A layer of rock through which sizeable amounts of water can flow. Sandstone and porous limestones make the best aquifers because they are full of interconnected holes through which water flows. An aquifer may be underneath, on top of, or sandwiched between layers of less permeable rock which make it harder for the water to flow. In many dry areas of the

---

**FACTS ABOUT AQUIFERS**

■ The Ogallala aquifer in the USA contains four trillion tonnes of water.
■ Water in the limestone aquifers of Romania has been there for 25,000 years.

---

world aquifers are very important for drinking water and irrigation. More water can be extracted by using **artesian wells**.

**See also**: *permeable and impermeable rocks.*

## arable farming

Arable farmers concentrate on growing **crops**, rather than keeping animals. Major arable farming areas have flat land and fertile, well-drained soil. Crops need less attention than animals, so on a mixed farm the crops will be planted in the fields furthest from the farm centre.

## arch

A natural formation caused by **erosion**, where the land looks like an arch or bridge. At sea, an arch is formed where waves erode two caves on a head-land until the backs meet and break through. On land, wind or water erosion can create a natural bridge spanning a valley or ravine.

**See also**: *coastal erosion.*

## archipelago

Volcanic islands formed either when a hot spot within the Earth's mantle produces a chain of volcanoes on the surface, such as the Hawaiian Archipelago, or at a destructive plate margin where the subduction of one plate beneath another produces an arc-shaped island group called an 'island arc', or **archipelago**, such as the Aleutian Archipelago. Novaya Zemlya in the Arctic Ocean, the northern extension of the Ural Mountains, resulted from continental flooding.

**See also:** *hot spot, plate tectonics, seamount.*

## Arctic, the

The Arctic is the name given to the region lying north of the Arctic Circle. The boundary of the Arctic is disputed. The two most common limits are the Arctic Circle and the natural **treeline** boundary. Under this definition west-ern and northern Alaska, parts of Canada and Greenland are all included, but Iceland is not. There is no arctic continent; and the greater part of the area comprises the Arctic Ocean, which is the world's smallest ocean. Pack-ice floating on the Arctic Ocean occupies almost the entire region between the North Pole and the coasts of North America and Eurasia. In spring the pack-ice begins to break up into ice floes which are carried by the south-flowing Greenland Current to the **Atlantic Ocean**.

Permanent ice sheets and year-round snow cover are found in regions where average monthly temperatures remain below 0°C/32°F. On land areas where the temperature rises above freezing point in the summer months, a stunted, treeless **tundra** vegetation is found. Lichens, mosses, and grasses spring to life during the short summer, when there is a maximum of 24 hours of daylight at the summer solstice on the Arctic Circle and six months' constant light at the North Pole. About 1 million aboriginal people live in the arctic region. Animal species include reindeer, caribou, musk ox, polar bear, seal, and walrus. The birds are chiefly sea birds, such as petrels and cormorants, and most are migratory. There are no reptiles. Fish include trout, salmon, and cod.

The Arctic is rich in coal, oil, and natural gas, and mineral resources including gold, silver, copper, uranium, lead, zinc, nickel, and bauxite.

## arête
A sharp, narrow ridge separating two glacial valleys or **corries**. Arêtes are common in glaciated mountain regions such as the Rockies, the Himalayas, and the Alps.

**See also**: *glacier and glaciation.*

## aridity
A region that receives less than 250 mm/10 in of rainfall each year, suffers from aridity. Little vegetation grows in these areas, and water shortage is a constant problem for people who live there. The most arid regions are called **deserts**. Arid regions exist in North Africa, Pakistan, Australia, and the USA.

## artesian well
A well that is filled with water rising naturally from an **aquifer**. An artesian well may be drilled into an aquifer to access the water, if the aquifer is sur-rounded by impermeable rocks. Artesian wells can become unreliable if over-used. They can also become polluted if pesticides or nitrates from the land seep into aquifers.

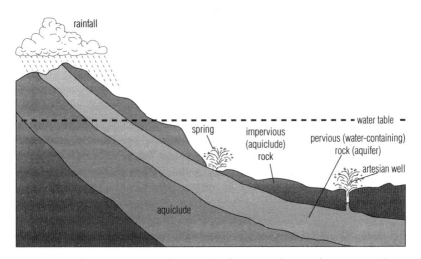

**artesian well** *In an artesian well, water rises from an underground water-containing rock layer under its own pressure. Rain falls at one end of the water-bearing layer, or aquifer, and percolates through the layer. The layer fills with water up to the level of the water table. Water will flow from a well under its own pressure if the well head is below the level of the water table.*

## Asia

Asia is the largest continent, made up of 50 countries, including China, Russia, and India, with a total population of 3,400 million.

Asia can be divided into five broad zones: northern, highland, arid, tropical, and insular. It is a continent of contrasts, containing both the highest point on the Earth's surface (Mount Everest, at 8,872 m/29,118 ft) and the lowest (the Dead Sea, at –394 m/–1,293 ft below sea level). Important rivers include the Yangtze and Yellow River. The Caspian Sea is the largest **lake** in the world. There are also large areas of **desert**, including the Gobi. The climate shows great extremes and contrasts, the heart of the continent becoming bitterly cold in winter and extremely hot in summer. Heavy monsoon rains affect all of southeast Asia between May and October.

The fertile eastern lowlands and river plains are one of the most densely populated regions in the world, with 1,500 million inhabitants, many of them living in large cities such as Tokyo and Osaka. In Asiatic Russia are the largest areas of **taiga** in the world.

Around 62% of Asia's population are employed in agriculture; and Asia

## WILDLIFE OF ASIA

- The northernmost zone of Asia, the **tundra**, bears only sparse and stunted vegetation and has permanently frozen subsoil (**permafrost**). The reindeer is one of the few permanent residents. The principal large hoofed animal of the tundra is the elk. Carnivores include the brown bear, wolf, wolverine, and arctic fox, as well as the marten and sable. Rodents include lemmings and flying squirrels.
- The tundra merges into the taiga, a belt of mainly coniferous forest reaching across the continent to form the largest continuous block of forest in the world. Approaching the Pacific coast, the character of the taiga gradually changes to a mixture of deciduous trees, comparable to the broad-leaved woodlands of Europe. Among the animals of this region are some that resemble those of Europe, others from various parts of Asia. They include several species of deer, bear, leopard, even a monkey (the Japanese macaque). The tiger – largest and most powerful of living carnivores – probably originated in this region before radiating south and west to its present restricted range.
- South of the tundra, forest gives way to treeless steppe, the Asian equivalent of prairie, where key mammals are burrowing rodents such as marmots and lemmings. They are the principal prey for a host of predatory animals and birds. At one time the steppe carried immense herds of herbivores including wild ass, wild horse, wild camel, saiga antelope, and goitred gazelle, but as the grasslands are also utilized with increasing intensity by pastoral humans and their domestic livestock, the wild species have inevitably declined, some almost to the point of extinction.
- The high **plateau** of Central Asia is home to several species that are distinguished by their adaptation to severe cold. Mammals include the Tibetan gazelle, wild ass, the snow leopard, and its principal prey the bharal or blue sheep. Of particular interest are the wild yak and the Tibetan antelope, or chiru, which habitually live at heights of up to 6,100 m/20,000 ft above sea-level, higher than any other large mammal. The giant panda lives in the Tibetan plateau.
- To the south of the Himalayas live lions, cheetah, elephant, and rhinoceros, while the tropical forests are inhabited by many species of monkey.

produces 46% of the world's cereal crops (91% of the world's rice). Other crops include mangoes, groundnuts, copra, rubber, tobacco, flax, jute, cotton, and silk. Fish, tungsten, tin, and oil are also economically important.

Asia's geographical location and its links not only with Europe but in the recent past with Africa, North America, and Australasia have provided abundant opportunities for plant and animal colonization. Thus the Asiatic fauna includes species having close affinities with neighbouring continents.

- wild sheep common to both Asia and North America
- elk, lynx, wolf, and wolverine common to Europe, Asia, and Canada
- pangolins and prosimians, as well as the cheetah, leopard, and lion common to Asia and Africa.

## asthenosphere
A layer within Earth's mantle lying beneath the lithosphere, typically beginning at a depth of approximately 100 km/63 mi and extending to depths of approximately 260 km/160 mi. Sometimes referred to as the 'weak sphere', it is characterized by being weaker and more elastic than the surrounding mantle.

The asthenosphere's elastic behaviour and ability to flow allow the overlying, more rigid plates of lithosphere to move laterally in a process known as **plate tectonics**.

## Atlantic Ocean
Saltiest of the main oceans, and with the greatest tidal range, the Atlantic links Europe and Africa in the east with the Americas in the west. Divided by the Equator into the North and South Atlantic, on average it is 3 km/2 mi deep. Fishing for herring and cod is important on both the American and European sides of the North Atlantic.

- *Physical features* The Atlantic basin covers 81,500,000 sq km/ 31,500,000 sq mi. Including the Arctic Ocean and Antarctic seas, the Atlantic covers a total of 106,200,000 sq km/41,000,000 sq mi. Its greatest depth is at the Milwaukee Depth in the Puerto Rico Trench at 8,648 m/28,374 ft. The **Mid-Atlantic Ridge** divides it from north to south. Lava welling up from this central area annually increases the distance between South America and Africa.

- *Currents* A warm equatorial current emerges from the Gulf of Mexico as the **Gulf Stream**, and has an enormous warming influence on the climate of northwest Europe. A cold current flows south from the Arctic Ocean. There is an area of calm known as the Sargasso Sea, in which extensive banks of weed float.

- *Islands and drainage* Continental islands are numerous, including the British Isles, the West Indies, Newfoundland, and the Falklands. Among the oceanic islands are Iceland, the Azores, Ascension, Tristan da Cunha, the Bermudas, the Canaries, the Cape Verdes, Madeira, Fernando Noronha, Trindade, and St Helena. The Atlantic Ocean receives the drainage of almost all western Europe, most of Africa, North America east of the Rocky Mountains, and South America east of the Andes. The chief river systems flowing into it are those of the Loire, Tagus, Senegal, Niger, Congo, St Lawrence, Mississippi, Orinoco, Amazon, and Río de La Plata.

- *Temperature and salinity* The surface temperature varies from about 30°C/86°F at the Equator to 4°C/39°F in the north and south temperate regions. The lower water temperatures average about 1–2°C/34–36°F. The water is saltiest in the trade-wind regions, and is always saltier below the surface.

- *Navigation* The Atlantic is heavily used by shipping, and floating ice is a real danger, as it interferes with the route between northern Europe and North America.

## atmosphere

The mixture of gases surrounding a planet, prevented from escaping by the pull of gravity. Earth's atmosphere is made up of nitrogen (78%), oxygen (21%) and argon (1%). Small quantities of other gases are also present, including water and carbon dioxide. The atmosphere is important in the water, carbon, and nitrogen cycles of nature. It is the main source of nitrogen, oxygen, and argon for use in industry.

The Earth's atmosphere is divided into four regions classified by temperature.

- *Troposphere (0 to 10 km/6 mi)* This lowest layer of the atmosphere is heated to an average temperature of 15°C/59°F by the Earth, which in turn is warmed by infrared and visible radiation from the Sun. Warm air cools as it rises in the troposphere and this rising of warm air causes rain and most other **weather** phenomena. The top of the troposphere is approximately –60°C/–140°F.

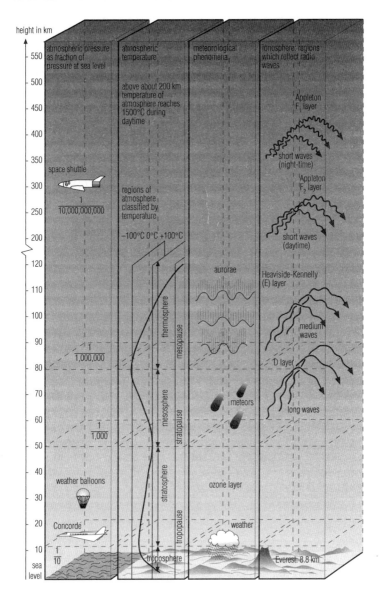

height in km

- 550    atmospheric pressure | atmospheric | meteorological | ionosphere: regions
         as fraction of | temperature | phenomena | which reflect radio
         pressure at sea level | | | waves

- 500

above about 200 km
temperature of
atmosphere reaches
- 450    1500°C during       Appleton
         daytime             F₁ layer

- 400

- 350    space shuttle                     short waves
                                           (night-time)

- 300    ✈                                 Appleton
         1                                 F₂ layer
- 250    ─────────           regions of
         10,000,000,000      atmosphere
                             classified by
- 200                        temperature      short waves
                                               (daytime)
                             −100°C 0°C +100°C

- 120                                 aurorae    Heaviside-Kennelly
                                                 (E) layer
- 110

- 100                    thermosphere              medium
                                                   waves
- 90     1              mesopause
         ─────────
         1,000,000                      D layer
- 80

- 70                    mesosphere         meteors    long waves

- 60     1             stratopause
         ─────
         1,000
- 50

- 40                    stratosphere

- 30     weather balloons                  ozone layer

         🎈

- 20     Concorde       tropopause              weather

         ✈
- 10     1                                               Everest: 8.8 km
         ──
         10
sea              troposphere
level

**atmosphere**  *All but 1% of the Earth's atmosphere lies in a layer reaching 30 km/19 mi above the ground. At a height of 5,500 m/18,000 ft, the air pressure is half that at sea level. The temperature of the atmosphere varies greatly with height; this produces a series of layers, called the troposphere, stratosphere, mesosphere, and thermosphere.*

- *Stratosphere (10–50 km/6–31 mi)* Temperature increases in the stratosphere, from –60°C/–140°F at the bottom to near 0°C/32°F at the top. The **ozone layer** at the top of the stratosphere prevents lethal amounts of ultraviolet radiation from reaching the Earth's surface.

- *Mesosphere (50–80 km/31–50 mi)* Temperature again decreases with altitude through the mesosphere, from 0°C/32°F to below –100°C/–212°F.

- *Thermosphere (80–700 km/50–435 mi)* In the highest layer temperature rises with altitude. The aurora borealis (northern lights) and the aurora australis (southern lights) occur in thermosphere.

---

**EARTH'S ATMOSPHERE IS LINKED TO EARTH'S GEOLOGY**

The chemistry of atmospheres is related to geology. Unlike Earth, Venus's dense atmosphere is dominantly carbon dioxide ($CO_2$). The carbon dioxide-rich atmosphere absorbs infrared radiation causing very high surface temperatures by the **greenhouse effect**. On Earth, the existence of liquid water enables carbonate rock such as **limestone** to form. If all of the carbon dioxide that has gone to form carbonate rock were liberated into the Earth's troposphere, our atmosphere would be similar to that of Venus.

---

**See also**: *greenhouse effect, ozone layer.*

### atmospheric circulation
The large-scale movement of air within the lower **atmosphere**.

- Warm air at the **Equator** rises, creating a zone of low pressure.

- This air moves towards the poles, losing energy and becoming cooler and denser, until it sinks back to the surface at around 30° **latitude**, creating an area of high pressure.

- At the surface, air moves from this high pressure zone back towards the low pressure zone at the Equator, completing a circulatory movement.

### atoll
A ring-shaped island, which may be broken or complete, made of coral and surrounding a **lagoon**. Thousands of atolls are found in the Pacific Ocean.

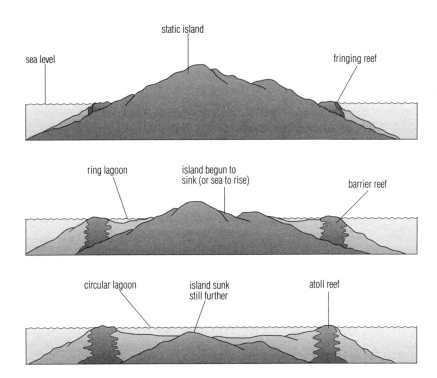

**atoll** *Coral atoll. The atoll is formed as a volcanic island gradually sinks. The reefs fringing the island build up as the island sinks, eventually producing a ring of coral (atoll) around the spot where the island sank.*

## attrition

Attrition is what happens when rock particles being carried by rivers, the sea, ice, or wind rub against each other and wear down, gradually becoming smaller and smaller. It is in this way that boulders are eventually reduced to sand.

**See also**: *coastal erosion.*

## Australasia

Australasia is the name given to some of the islands of the South Pacific, including Australia, New Zealand, and Papua New Guinea. Australia is the largest of these countries, with a population of 17 million, most of whom live in the coastal cities of Sydney, Perth, Melbourne, Brisbane, and Adelaide. The population of New Zealand is 3.5 million, many of whom live in Auckland.

The Australian climate is very hot and dry, and the central part of the country consists of desert known as the outback. Ayers Rock, in the centre of this region, is the world's largest monolith. Mount Kosciusko in New South Wales is Australia's highest peak, at 2,229 m/7,316 ft. The Great Barrier Reef, off the northeast coast of Australia is the longest **coral reef** in the world. Australia has few rivers, the longest being the Murray-Darling, in the southeast. New Zealand comprises two islands. North Island has a warm climate and volcanic geysers are found there. The climate of South Island is less warm, but humid, and the landscape includes snow-capped mountains and deep fjords. In the fjord country, magnificent forests of southern beech are found.

The gum tree grows widely in Australia. It can thrive in a very wide range of habitats, with shrubby species which form areas of scrub, and trees which completely dominate the forests of the winter-rain regions. Gum trees cannot grow in desert, where few plants except the salt bush and blue bush can grow.

Australasia's manufacturing sector supplies goods for the home market. There is also a large export-oriented sector, based on exports of agricultural or mineral products.

Australia is the only country in which marsupials such as kangaroos, wallabies, and koalas have evolved freely. Crocodiles inhabit the humid swamplands of northern Australia. The emu also lives in Australia, and the cassowary in New Guinea. Both these bird species are flightless.

The islands of Southeast Asia form a number of seismically and volcanically active island arcs. This area is one where three crustal plates meet,

---

**AUSTRALASIAN INDUSTRIES**

| Country | Produces |
| --- | --- |
| Australia | bauxite, nickel, silver, cobalt, gold, iron ore, diamonds, lead, uranium, wool, mutton, lamb, copra, palm oil, coffee, cocoa |
| New Zealand | lamb, wool, butter, cheese |
| Papua New Guinea | gold, copper, rubber |

with complex geological results. The area has been active since the late Palaeozoic period, and activity continues to the present day.

The present land mass of New Zealand came into being with the uplift of new mountain ranges during the Cretaceous period, though the western part of the country contains older Palaeozoic metamorphic rocks. The Alpine Fault of New Zealand is an important fault which runs northeast through eastern New Zealand and has been active since late Mesozoic times up to the present day. Volcanic activity continued through the Tertiary along the east side of South Island. In North Island volcanic rocks erupted in recent times along the still active central volcanic belt.

## avalanche

A mass of snow and ice that falls rapidly down a mountainside. The snow compacts into ice as it moves, and may sweep rocks along with it, causing more damage. Avalanches are particularly dangerous in ski resort areas, such as the French Alps. One positive effect of an avalanche can be its slide tracks, long gouges down the mountainside that clear the land of snow and forest and enable plants that cannot tolerate shade to regrow and create wildlife corridors.

**WHAT CAUSES AN AVALANCHE**

Snow is unstable when it settles on mountain slopes, especially on slopes of 35° or more. Various changes can trigger an avalanche, including:

- a rise in temperature
- sudden sounds
- earth-borne vibrations.

## badlands

A barren landscape cut by **erosion** into a maze of ravines, pinnacles, gullies and sharp-edged ridges. Areas in South Dakota and Nebraska, USA, are examples. Badlands, which can be created by overgrazing, are so called because of their total lack of value for agriculture and their inaccessibility.

## backwash

After a wave breaks on a **beach**, it is drawn back towards the sea as backwash. The water rushing up the beach when a wave breaks is called **swash**.
**See also**: *beach, coastal erosion.*

## barometer

An instrument used to forecast the weather by measuring the air pressure. Rising pressure means that the weather will become calmer, falling pressure shows storms on the way. (*See illustration on p. 24.*)

## barrage

A structure built across a river or estuary in order to manage the water. The Thames barrier, London, UK is an example of a **flood** control barrage. A barrage may be used to regulate the water supply by controlling floods or storing water for **irrigation**, or to generate power by, for example, harnessing wave energy in estuaries.

## basalt

Commonest volcanic **igneous rock**. Earth's ocean floor is virtually entirely made of basalt. Basaltic lava tends to be runny and flows for great distances before solidifying. Successive eruptions of basalt have formed the great plateaus of Colorado and the Deccan plateau region of southwest India. In some places, such as Fingal's Cave in the Inner Hebrides of Scotland, shrink-

Basalt is the commonest rock in the solar system.
Much of the surfaces of the terrestrial planets, Mercury, Venus, Earth, and Mars, as well as the Moon are composed of basalt.

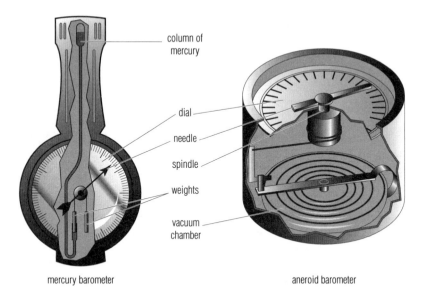

mercury barometer                                          aneroid barometer

**barometer** *In the mercury barometer (left), the weight of the column of mercury is balanced by the pressure of the atmosphere on the lower end. A change in height of the column indicates a change in atmospheric pressure. In the aneroid barometer (right), any change of air pressure makes the vacuum chamber expand or contract slightly. These movements are transferred to a pointer and scale by a chain of levers.*

age during the solidification of the molten lava caused the formation of hexagonal columns.

Basalt is usually dark grey but can also be green, brown, or black. Its essential constituent minerals are calcium-rich feldspar and calcium and magnesium-rich pyroxene.

## beach

A strip of land bordering the sea, consisting of boulders and pebbles or sand. Beaches are formed by **coastal erosion**. Sand and pebbles are carried along the beach in a zigzag pattern by **longshore drift**. Erosion follows a natural cycle, with winter storms and high spring tides taking sand away from the shore. In summer, calmer seas bring sand back to the beach. Beaches may be damaged by:

- natural erosion
- commercial extraction of sand and aggregate

- removal of mineral deposits
- pollution from oil spills or sewage.

  **See also**: *groyne, longshore drift.*

## Beaufort scale

A system of measuring the speed of the wind, by looking at the effect the wind is having on natural objects such as trees. The scale ranges from 0 to 17. A zero reading means complete calm, while 12 indicates a hurricane. Measurements of 13–17 show degrees of hurricane force. The scale was devised in 1806 by British hydrographer Francis Beaufort (1774–1857).

| Number and description | Features | Air speed | |
|---|---|---|---|
| | | kph | mph |
| 0 calm | smoke rises vertically; water smooth | 0–2 | 0–1 |
| 1 light air | smoke shows wind direction; water ruffled | 2–5 | 1–3 |
| 2 light breeze | leaves rustle; wind felt on face | 6–11 | 4–7 |
| 3 gentle breeze | loose paper blows around | 12–19 | 8–12 |
| 4 moderate breeze | branches sway | 20–29 | 13–18 |
| 5 fresh breeze | small trees sway, leaves blown off | 30–39 | 19–24 |
| 6 strong breeze | whistling in telephone wires; sea spray from waves | 40–50 | 25–31 |
| 7 near gale | large trees sway | 51–61 | 32–38 |
| 8 gale | twigs break from trees | 62–74 | 39–46 |
| 9 strong gale | branches break from trees | 75–87 | 47–54 |
| 10 storm | trees uprooted; weak buildings collapse | 88–101 | 55–63 |
| 11 violent storm | widespread damage | 102–117 | 64–73 |
| 12 hurricane | widespread structural damage | above 118 | above 74 |

## bed

A single **sedimentary rock** layer with a distinct set of physical characteristics or fossils, readily distinguishable from those of beds above and below. Layers of successive beds are called strata. Beds or strata are separated by well-defined surfaces called bedding planes.

The depth of a bed can vary from a fraction of a centimetre to several metres or yards, and can extend over any area. The term is also used to indicate the floor beneath a body of water (lake bed) and a layer formed by a fall of particles (ash bed).

## biodegradable

Items such as food waste and paper that can be broken down by bacteria. This is a natural process which reduces the waste materials to a liquid, producing nutrients that are recycled into the **ecosystem**. One disadvantage of biodegrading is that it produces methane, an explosive greenhouse gas. At some waste tips, methane is drawn off into underground pipes and used as a cheap energy source. It is very difficult to dispose of nonbiodegradable substances, such as glass, heavy metals, and most types of plastic.

## biodiversity

The huge variety of animal, plant, and microbiological life that exists on the **Earth**, and the numerous different ecosystems where these organisms live. It is very important to maintain **biodiversity**, as the loss of one part of the system affects many others. For example, the destruction of **rainforests** has meant that many plant and animal species have also been lost, since they have nowhere else to live.

---

### FACTS ABOUT BIODIVERSITY

■ It is hard to estimate how many species exist because habitats such as tropical forests have not been fully explored.
■ No more than 10% of bacteria have been identified.
■ Between half and three-quarters of the world's biodiversity lives on just 7% of the Earth's surface.
■ Attempts to make industrialized countries work towards preserving biodiversity have not been totally successful.

---

## biomass

The total weight of organisms living in a particular area, either for a certain species, such as earthworms, or for a general category, like herbivores. For animals and plants, biomass is measured by multiplying the total number, by the weight of one unit. Biomass measurements are used to study:

• interactions between different organisms
• changes in those interactions
• population changes.

Biomass is also used to measure energy. About two-thirds of the world's population cooks and heats water by burning biomass, usually wood. Plant biomass is a renewable source of energy as new supplies can be grown quickly. Fossil fuels, originally formed from biomass, are not renewable, because they take so long to accumulate.

## biome
A major geographical area, characterized by its animal and plant life, and its climate. There are eight terrestrial biomes:

- **tundra**
- **temperate deciduous forest**
- **temperate grasslands**
- **desert**
- **taiga**
- **chaparral**
- **tropical grasslands**
- **tropical rainforest.**

## biosphere
The narrow zone capable of supporting life on this planet, encompassing a fraction of the **Earth's** crust, its waters, and the lower regions of the **atmosphere**. All of the Earth's ecosystems are within the biosphere.

## biotechnology
The use of living organisms to manufacture food, drugs, or other products. Brewing and baking, which rely on yeast fermentation, are traditional examples of biotechnology. The dairy industry uses bacteria and fungi to make cheese and yogurt from milk.

---

### DEVELOPMENTS IN BIOTECHNOLOGY

Antibiotics have been made since the 1940s, by fermenting moulds.
In genetic engineering single-celled organisms are used to make drugs and vaccines.

---

## biotic factor
The influence of a living variable on an **ecosystem**, e.g. the changing population of elephants and its effect on the African savanna.

## biotic potential
The total theoretical reproductive capacity of an individual organism or

species under ideal environmental conditions. The biotic potential of many small organisms such as bacteria, annual plants and small mammals is very high but rarely reached, as other elements of the ecosystem such as predators, nutrient availability, keep the population growth in check.

## birth rate

A birth rate of 2% (sometimes expressed as 20 per thousand), means that for every thousand people in the population, 20 babies are born each year. This figure includes the whole population, including men and women who are too old to bear children, and so is sometimes called the crude birth rate. In industrial countries birth rates have fallen because:

- contraception methods have improved
- more people use contraception
- living standards are better.

   **See also**: *demographic transition.*

## Countries with the highest birth rates*

| Region/country | Crude birth rate (per 1,000 population) (1977) |
|---|---|
| Afghanistan | 53 |
| Niger | 50 |
| Angola | 48 |
| Ethiopia | 48 |
| Congo, Democratic Republic of | 45 |
| Burundi | 43 |
| Ghana | 38 |
| Kenya | 37 |
| Nepal | 37 |
| Lesotho | 36 |
| Pakistan | 36 |
| Sudan | 34 |
| Cambodia | 34 |

*Birth-rate data are for live births.

## blowhole

An air passage leading from a sea cave to the cliffs. Every time a wave rushes into the cave, increased pressure forces water up and out through the opening, causing a spurt of water to appear on the cliff top.

   **See also**: *coastal erosion.*

## blow-out

A hollow or depression of bare sand in an area of **dunes** on which vegetation grows. Blow-outs are common in coastal dune complexes and are formed by wind erosion, which can be triggered by:

- destruction of small areas of vegetation by people or animals
- lack of sand supply from a beach
- localized dryness.

## bog

An area of flat wetland, where there is a great deal of water containing very little oxygen. This slows down decomposition, so that dead plants gradually turn into peat. There are large bogs in Ireland and northern Scotland. Typical plants found in bogs include:

- sphagnum moss
- rushes
- cotton grass
- heathers
- insect-eating plants, such as sundews and bladderworts.

## braiding

The subdivision of a **river** into an interlacing network of channels, islets, and bars caused by deposition of sediment. Braiding often develops when a river or stream carrying a great deal of eroded material emerges from mountain topography. The change in gradient causes the river to slow down and drop part of its suspended material. Braided channels are common in meltwater streams at the foot of **glaciers**.

## caldera

A very large, basin-shaped crater, found at the top of a **volcano**, where the original peak has collapsed into an empty chamber beneath. A caldera is many times larger than the original volcanic vent. It may be flooded, producing a crater lake, or the flat floor may contain a number of small volcanic cones.

## canal

An artificial waterway built for drainage, **irrigation**, or navigation. The first major canal in the UK was the Bridgewater Canal, 1759–61, constructed for the 3rd Duke of Bridgewater to carry coal from his collieries to Manchester, England. Many disused canals have been restored for the use of pleasure craft. Where speed is not a prime factor, the cost-effectiveness of transporting goods by canal has encouraged a revival; Belgium, France, Germany, and the states of the former USSR are among countries that have extended and streamlined their canals.

- *Navigation and ship canals* often link rivers or sea inlets to form a waterway system. The Suez Canal in 1869 and the Panama Canal in 1914 eliminated long trips around continents and dramatically shortened shipping routes. Inland canals are usually built following the contours of the land. When the land rises, locks are used to raise the level of the water.

- *Irrigation canals* carry water for irrigation from rivers, reservoirs, or wells, and are designed to maintain an even flow of water over the whole length. The River Nile has fed canals to maintain life in Egypt since the earliest times. Excessive extraction of water for irrigation from rivers and lakes can cause environmental damage.

## canyon

A very deep mountain valley with sides that are almost vertical. Canyons are formed by streams or rivers down-cutting, usually in dry or cold areas, where little sediment is deposited, and the sides of the canyon remain steep. There are many canyons in the western USA and in Mexico such as:

- the Grand Canyon of the Colorado River in Arizona
- the canyon in Yellowstone National Park
- the Black Canyon in Colorado.

## carrying capacity

The maximum number of animals of a given species that a particular area can support. When a species exceeds carrying capacity, the population may be reduced by emigration, reproductive failure, or starvation.

---

**FACTORS AFFECTING CARRYING CAPACITY**

- availability of food
- amount of space and light
- competition for food and space from other species
- disease
- number of predators.

---

## cash crop

Crop grown for export rather than for the people's own use, for example, coffee, cotton, or sugar beet. Many Third World countries grow cash crops in order to repay their debts, rather than growing food for their own population. The price paid for cash crops depends on financial interests, such as those of the multinational companies and the International Monetary Fund.

- In 1990 Uganda, Rwanda, Nicaragua, and Somalia were the countries most dependent on cash crops for income.
- In Britain, the most widespread cash crop is the potato.

    **See also**: *crops*.

## catch crop

In **crop rotation**, a crop such as turnip that is inserted between two principal crops in order to provide some quick livestock feed or soil improvement at a time when the land would otherwise be lying idle.

- In the gap between harvesting a crop of winter-sown wheat and sowing a spring variety of barley, for example, an additional catch crop of turnips or ryegrass can be produced for animal feed in the late winter period when other green fodder is scarce. When the catch crop is ploughed under, the succeeding spring crop benefits from the improvement to the soil.

- Catch crops are only suited to lighter soils where stock can be brought in winter without damage.

**See also**: *crops.*

## catchment area

An area from which water flows into a river. A catchment area can also mean an area served by a facility such as a hospital or school.

## cave

Roofed-over cavity in the ground or in cliffs, usually produced by the action of underground water or waves.

---

### FACTS ABOUT CAVES

- *Limestone caves* Most inland caves are found in **limestone** rock, because it dissolves in water. The passage of water enlarges the joints, fissures, and bedding planes into caves which eventually join to form a complex network. Limestone caves are usually found just below the water table, wherever limestone outcrops on the surface. The biggest cave in the world is over 70 km/43 mi long, at Holloch, Switzerland.
- *Sea caves* Coastal caves are formed where relatively soft rock or rock containing weaknesses, is exposed to severe wave action. The gouging (corrasion) and solution (**corrosion**) of weaker, more soluble rock layers, plus the effects of subsidence, create hollows in the rock.
- *Celebrated caves* include: the Mammoth Cave in Kentucky, USA, 6.4 km/4 mi long and 38 m/125 ft high; the Caverns of Adelsberg (Postumia) near Trieste, Italy, which extend for many miles; Carlsbad Cave, New Mexico, the largest in the USA; the Cheddar Caves, England; Fingal's Cave, Scotland, which has a range of basalt columns; and Peak Cavern, England.

---

**See also**: *blowhole, stalactites, stalagmites.*

## cavitation

The **erosion** of rocks caused by the forcing of air into cracks. Cavitation results from the pounding of waves on the coast and the swirling of turbulent river currents. The process is particularly common at waterfalls, where the turbulent falling water contains many air bubbles, which burst to send shock waves into the rocks of the river bed and banks.

## census

Official count of the population of a country, usually undertaken by the government. In the UK, a census has been conducted every ten years since 1801, although the census may become unnecessary as computerized databanks develop. The information was originally used for military call-up and taxation. Later, as other information regarding age, sex, and occupation of each individual was included, it became used for planning. Governments can use census information to assess future needs in areas such as health, education, transport, and housing.

## central business district (CBD)

Area of a town or city dominated by shops, offices, entertainment venues, and local-government buildings where most of the commercial activity takes place. Characteristically, the CBD has high rents and rates, tall buildings, chain stores, and easy pedestrian access. It is located where transport links meet and is often found in the historic centre of a city.

## CFC (chlorofluorocarbon)

A class of nontoxic, nonflammable, odourless, and chemically inert synthetic chemicals, widely used as aerosol propellants, refrigerants, degreasers, and in the manufacture of foam packaging. Popular since the 1930s, there is now concern that CFCs damage the **ozone layer**.

When CFCs are released into the atmosphere, they drift up slowly into

**FACTS ABOUT CFCS**

- CFCs can remain in the atmosphere for more than 100 years.
- Research into safe methods of destroying existing CFCs and developing replacements is being carried out.
- The use of CFCs is banned in many countries.

the stratosphere. Under the influence of ultraviolet radiation from the Sun, CFCs react with ozone ($O_3$) to form free chlorine (Cl) atoms and molecular oxygen ($O_2$), thereby destroying the ozone layer. The chlorine liberated during ozone breakdown can react with still more ozone, making the CFCs particularly dangerous to the environment.

**See also**: *greenhouse effect.*

## chalk

Soft, fine-grained, whitish sedimentary rock extensively quarried for use in cement, lime, and mortar, and in the manufacture of cosmetics and toothpaste. Chalk is primarily made of the calcium carbonate remains of microscopic marine plants, and is formed from deposits of deep-sea sediments. Chalk covers a wide area in Europe. In England it stretches in a belt from Wiltshire and Dorset across Buckinghamshire and Cambridgeshire to Lincolnshire and Yorkshire, and also forms the North and South Downs, and the cliffs of south and southeast England.

**See also**: *rock.*

## chaos theory

A branch of mathematics that attempts to explain irregular systems such as the weather, the behaviour of which is difficult to predict because it is influenced by so many unknown factors. Chaos theory tries to predict the probable behaviour of the weather by using a rapid calculation of the impact of as wide a range of elements as possible. It emerged in the 1970s with the development of sophisticated computers.

**See also**: *meteorology.*

## chaparral

An area dominated by thick scrub, thorny bushes, and low-growing trees, found in the southwestern USA. These are areas of low rainfall, and the vegetation tends to be evergreen and resistant to droughts.

## chlorofluorocarbon

Usually referred to as **CFC**.

## city

A large and important town. Cities cover only 2% of the Earth's surface but use 75% of all resources. In April 1996, the World Resources Report predicted that two-thirds of the world's population will live in cities by 2025. Cities with more than 10 million inhabitants are sometimes referred to as megacities.

## Cities with a population greater than 10 million

| Rank | City | Population (millions) 1996 |
|------|------|----------------------------|
| 1 | Tokyo, Japan | 27.2 |
| 2 | Mexico City, Mexico | 16.9 |
| 3 | São Paulo, Brazil | 16.8 |
| 4 | New York (NY), USA | 16.4 |
| 5 | Bombay, India | 15.7 |
| 6 | Shanghai, China | 13.7 |
| 7 | Los Angeles (CA), USA | 12.6 |
| 8 | Calcutta, India | 12.1 |
| 9 | Buenos Aires, Argentina | 11.9 |
| 10 | Seoul, South Korea | 11.8 |
| 11 | Beijing, China | 11.4 |
| 12 | Lagos, Nigeria | 10.9 |
| 13 | Osaka, Japan | 10.6 |
| 14= | Delhi, India | 10.3 |
|  | Rio de Janeiro, Brazil | 10.3 |
| 16 | Karachi, Pakistan | 10.1 |

*Source*: United Nations Population Division, Department of Economic and Social Affairs.

## clay

A very fine-grained sedimentary **rock** that can take up large amounts of water. Clay can be moulded when wet, and when heated hardens and becomes impermeable. It may be white, grey, red, yellow, blue, or black, depending on its composition, and is used in pottery and for making bricks. Types of clay include: alluvial, building, brick, china, fireclay, puddle clay.

## cliff

A steep rock face which may be up to 1,000 m/3,000 ft high. The height is affected by:

- the type of material forming the cliff. Granite, for example, can support a much higher cliff than clay

- the position of layers of weak rock. If these are near the foot of the cliff, the cliff will be weakened and may collapse.

## climate

Combination of weather conditions at a particular place over a period of at least 30 years. An area's climate is classified by measuring averages, extremes, and frequencies of temperature, atmospheric pressure, **precipitation**, **wind**, humidity, and sunshine. The factors that influence an area's climate are its:

- latitude and longitude
- closeness to the sea and prevailing ocean currents
- height above sea level
- type of soil and vegetation
- wind belts and air masses
- topography.

Climatologists are especially concerned with the influence of human activity on climate change, among the most important of which are those currently linked with **ozone** depleters and the **greenhouse effect**.

Many different systems of classifying climate have been devised. Commonly, vegetation-based classifications, such as desert, tundra, and rainforest, are used in conjunction with classification by air mass, linking the climate of an area with the movement of the air masses it experiences. Due to the rotation of the Earth, there are three convection cells in each hemisphere. These include:

- two cells in which air rises at the Equator and sinks at latitudes north and south of the tropics
- two cells at the mid-latitudes, where the rising air from the sub-tropics flows towards the cold air masses of the polar regions
- two cells circulating from the two polar regions.

These six main circulating cells produce seven terrestrial zones – three rainy regions at the Equator and the temperate latitudes which result from moisture-laden rising air, and four dry or desert regions at the poles and sub-tropics resulting from the dry descending air.

**See also**: *climatic change, meteorology, rain, weather.*

### climatic change
Change in the climate of an area or of the whole world over an appreciable period of time. Climatic change may be caused by changes in the amount of energy coming from the sun. Other factors, such as **ozone** depletion, and increased amounts of dust in the atmosphere from volcanic eruptions, may also have an effect.

**See also**: *climate.*

## cloud

A mass of water vapour that floats in the atmosphere, having been formed when air cools and condenses into minute water particles. As well as being an essential part of the **hydrological cycle**, clouds are important in the regulation of radiation in the **atmosphere**. They reflect short-wave radiation from the sun, and absorb and re-emit long-wave radiation from the Earth's surface.

**See also**: *fog, mist.*

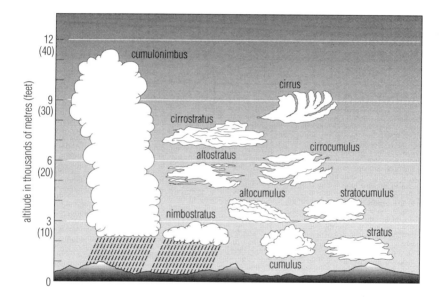

**cloud** *Clouds are classified according to the height at which they occur and their shape. Cirrus clouds occur at high levels and look like feathery white wisps. Cirrostratus stretch across the sky as a thin white sheet. Cirrocumulus clouds occur in rounded tufts, while altocumulus are similar but larger white clouds, sometimes arranged in lines. Altostratus are like heavy cirrostratus clouds and may stretch across the sky as a grey sheet. Stratocumulus clouds are generally lower and dull grey, giving a leaden sky that may not yield rain. Cumulus and cumulonimbus clouds are produced by ascending air currents. Stratus clouds form sheets parallel to the horizon and are like high fogs.*

## coal

A hard black mineral substance formed from compacted plant matter and used as a **fossil fuel**. Coal burning is one of the main causes of **acid rain**.

From the **industrial revolution** until the beginning of the 20th century, Britain was the largest coal producer in the world, but the USA now produces more. As the use of oil and nuclear energy has become more widespread, coal has become less popular as a fuel, and now accounts for only one-quarter of the world's energy.

Coal is classified according to the proportion of carbon it contains.

• *Anthracite* (shiny, with about 90% carbon) burns at high temperature with little smoke and is used domestically.

• *Bituminous coal* (shiny and dull patches, about 75% carbon) is the most common type of coal.

• *Lignite* (woody, grading into peat, about 50% carbon) is used to fuel power stations in some countries.

## coastal erosion

The wearing away of the land by the constant battering of the **sea's** waves. The main processes of coastal erosion are:

• hydraulic action, when waves compress air pockets in rocks and cliffs, the expanding air breaking the rocks apart

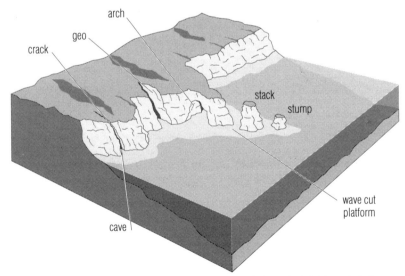

**coastal erosion** *Typical features of coastal erosion: from the initial cracks in less resistant rock through to arches, stacks, and stumps that can occur as erosion progresses.*

- **corrasion**
- **attrition**
- **corrosion**
- frost shattering (or freeze-thaw), caused by the expansion of frozen sea water in cavities
- biological weathering, caused by the burrowing of rock-boring molluscs.

Where resistant rocks form headlands, the sea erodes the coast in stages, forming **blowholes** and **arches**. When the roof of the arch collapses, a stack is formed.

**Beach** erosion occurs when more sand is eroded and carried away from the beach than is deposited by **longshore drift**. Some areas of coastline in Britain may be eroding at a rate of 6 m/20 ft per year. Current policy is to surrender the land to the sea, rather than build costly sea defences in rural areas.

## colonialism

Policy of extending the power and rule of a government beyond its own boundaries. A country may attempt to dominate others by direct rule and settlement, or by controlling markets for goods and raw materials.

Colonialism, also known as imperialism, has existed over the centuries. During the **industrial revolution** European countries looked to other countries for raw materials. Imperialists:

- claimed that they were expanding civilization to underdeveloped countries
- associated their military and technological strength with a belief in the racial and cultural superiority of Europeans over other races.

Anti-imperialist movements grew during the 1920s and 1930s, and by the middle of the century many former colonies had become independent.

## community

A collection of different kinds of plants, animals, and other organisms living within a particular area. Communities are usually named after a dominant feature, such as a type of plant – for example, a beechwood community, or a prominent physical feature – for example, a freshwater-pond community.

## condensation

The process that takes place when a vapour turns into a liquid. This often happens when the vapour comes into contact with a cold surface.

Condensation is the process by which water vapour turns into fine water droplets to form a **cloud**.

Condensation in the atmosphere occurs when the air becomes completely saturated with water vapour. As air rises it cools and contracts, and the cooler it becomes, the less water it can hold. Rain is frequently associated with warm weather fronts because the air rises and cools, allowing the water vapour to condense as rain.

**See also**: *rain*.

## confluence
The point at which two **rivers** join, or where a smaller river, called a tributary, joins a larger river.

## conifer
Evergreen tree, such as pine and fir, which grows quickly and can tolerate poor soil, steep slopes, and short growing seasons. Coniferous forests are widespread in Scandinavia and upland areas of the UK such as the Scottish Highlands, and are often planted in **afforestation** schemes. Conifers also grow in mixed woodland.

## conservation
Action taken to protect and preserve the natural world, usually from pollution, overexploitation, and other harmful features of human activity. The late 1980s saw a great increase in public concern for the environment, with membership of conservation groups, such as Friends of the Earth and Greenpeace, rising sharply. Globally the most important issues include:

- damage to the **ozone layer** by **CFCs** (**chlorofluorocarbons**)
- the build-up of carbon dioxide in the atmosphere, which contributes to the **greenhouse effect**
- **deforestation**.

## continent
Any one of the seven large land masses of the Earth:

- **Asia**
- **Africa**
- **North and South America**
- **Europe**

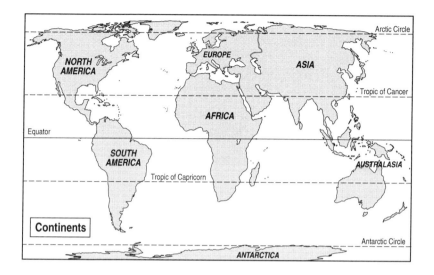

Continents

- **Australasia**
- **Antarctica.**

Continents are constantly moving and evolving by the movements of **plate tectonics**. A continent does not end at the coastline; its boundary is the edge of the shallow **continental shelf**, which may extend several hundred kilometres out to sea.

At the centre of each continental mass lies a shield or **craton**, a deformed mass of old **metamorphic** rocks dating from Precambrian times. The shield is thick, compact, and solid, having undergone all the mountain-building activity it is ever likely to, and is usually worn flat. The Canadian Shield is an example. Around the shield is a concentric pattern of **fold mountains**, with older ranges, such as the Rockies, closest to the shield, and younger ranges, such as the coastal ranges of North America, farther away. This general concentric pattern is modified when two continental masses have collided, and they become welded with a great mountain range along the join, the way Europe and northern Asia are joined along the Urals. If a continent is torn apart, the new continental edges have no fold mountains, but there is evidence of a **rift valley**; for instance, east coast of South America, where it tore away from Africa 200 million years ago.

**See also**: *continental climate, continental drift, continental shelf, plate tectonics.*

## continental climate

The type of climate typical of a large, mid-latitude land mass. Areas with a continental climate are a long way from the oceans, which affects their climate in two ways:

• The annual rainfall is very low because little atmospheric moisture is available.

• The temperature range is very large over a year, because the temperature-moderating effect of closeness to the sea has been lost. For example, at Yakutsk in eastern Asia average monthly temperatures range from −42°C/−107°F to 20°C/68°F.

## continental drift

The theory that, about 250–200 million years ago, the Earth consisted of a single large continent (Pangaea), which broke apart to form the continents known today. The theory was put forward in 1912 by Alfred Wegener, but such vast continental movements could not be satisfactorily explained until the theory of **plate tectonics** in the 1960s.

The term continental drift is not strictly correct, since land masses do not drift through the oceans. The Earth is covered with an armour of plates that fit together like the pieces of a jigsaw puzzle. Due to dynamic forces in the mantle the plates are in constant motion, and the continents are slowly changing and shifting their positions. Over 200 million years ago, the continents were part of one massive continent, Pangaea. By 200 million years ago, Pangaea had begun to rift apart. By 50 million years ago, the continents were approaching their present positions. (*See illustration on opposite page.*)

## continental rise

The portion of the ocean floor rising gently from the **abyssal plain** toward the steeper **continental slope**. The continental rise is a depositional feature formed from sediments transported down the slope. Much of the continental rise consists of coalescing submarine **alluvial fans** bordering the continental slope.

## continental shelf

A gently sloping plain that may extend several hundred kilometres under the sea from the edge of a continent. The continental shelf often contains large reserves of oil and gas. When the angle of the sea bed increases to 1°–5° it becomes known as the continental slope.

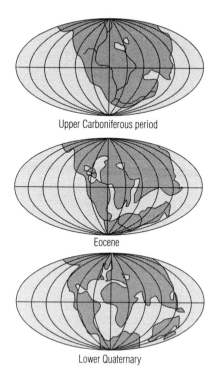

Upper Carboniferous period

Eocene

Lower Quaternary

**continental drift** *The continents are slowly shifting their positions, driven by fluid motion beneath the Earth's crust. Over 200 million years ago, there was a single large continent called Pangaea. By 200 million years ago, the continents had started to move apart. By 50 million years ago, the continets were approaching their present position.*

## continental slope

Slope that extends downward from the edge of the **continental shelf** at an angle of 1°–5°. In some places, such as south of the Aleutian Islands of Alaska, continental slopes extend directly to the ocean deeps or **abyssal plain**. In others, such as the east coast of North America, they grade into the gentler continental rises that in turn grade into the abyssal plains. Some continental slopes are cut by submarine canyons.

## contour

A line drawn on a map to join points of equal height. Contours are drawn at regular height intervals; for example, every 10 m. The closer together the lines are, the steeper the slope. Contour patterns on a map can be used to interpret the relief of an area and to identify land forms.

## conurbation
Large continuous built-up area formed when several neighbouring urban settlements merge together. Typically, conurbations have populations in excess of 1 million people and some are many times that size. The Osaka–Kobe conurbation in Japan, for example, contains over 16 million people.

## cooperative farming
System in which individual farmers pool their resources, except land, to buy commodities such as seeds and fertilizers, and services such as marketing. The system is found throughout the world and is particularly widespread in Denmark and the former Soviet republics. In a collective farm, land is also held in common.

## coral reef
Coral is a rock made up of the fused skeletons of tiny sea animals. Corals can only live in clear, warm water and are found in the Pacific and Indian Oceans. The rocks formed by coral can be very sharp, and may make a reef, or line of rocks, on or just beneath the surface of the water.

## core
The very centre of the **Earth**, divided into an outer core, which begins at a depth of 2,898 km/1,800 mi, and an inner core, which begins at a depth of 4,982 km/3,095 mi. Both parts are thought to consist of iron-nickel alloy. The outer core is liquid and the inner core is solid. The temperature of the core is thought to be at least 4,000°C/7,232°F, but remains controversial.

## corrasion
The main process of **erosion**, where solid rock surfaces are ground and battered away by rock particles in water, ice, and wind. As the eroding particles are carried along, they themselves become eroded by **attrition**.
  **See also**: *coastal erosion*.

## corrie
A steep-sided hollow in the mountainside of a **glaciated** area, formed in the Ice Age by glaciers as the weight and movement of the ice ground out the

bottom and wore back the sides. A corrie is open at the front, and its sides and back are formed of **arêtes**. There may be a lake in the bottom, called a tarn. A corrie is sometimes called a cirque or a cwm.

## corrosion

The process by which water dissolves rocks such as limestone. Chalk and limestone coasts are often broken down by corrosion (also called solution).

## crater

Bowl-shaped depression in the ground, usually round, with steep sides, formed by an explosion from:

- a volcano erupting
- a bomb
- the impact of a meteorite.

The Moon has more than 300,000 craters over 1 km/0.6 mi in diameter, formed by meteorite collisions. Similar craters on Earth have mostly been worn away by erosion.

Studies at the Jet Propulsion Laboratory in California, USA, have shown that craters produced by impact or by volcanic activity have distinctive shapes, enabling astronomers to distinguish likely methods of crater formation on planets in the Solar System. Unlike volcanic craters, impact craters have a raised rim and central peak and are almost always circular regardless of the meteorite's angle of incidence when it hit.

## craton or shield

The core of a continent, a vast tract of highly deformed **metamorphic rock** around which the continent has been built. Intense mountain-building periods shook these shield areas in Precambrian times before stable conditions set in. Cratons exist in the hearts of all the continents, a typical example being the Canadian Shield.

The rocks of a cratons were formed deep in the Earth's crust and are exposed because the region has undergone extensive **erosion**. Younger mountain ranges usually surround them.

## crevasse

Deep crack, which can be several metres deep, in the surface of a glacier. Crevasses often occur where a glacier flows over the break of a slope, because the upper layers of ice are unable to stretch and cracks result.

Crevasses may also form at the edges of glaciers owing to friction with the bedrock.

## crofting

The farming of common land cooperatively, in which the crofters (tenants) have the right of grazing on unenclosed hillsides. Although grazing land is still shared, arable land is usually enclosed.

## crop

Any plant grown or harvested by farmers. Over 80 crops are grown world-wide, providing food and supplying fibres, rubber, pharmaceuticals, dyes, and other materials.

---

### MAIN GROUPS OF CROPS

- *Food crops* provide the bulk of people's food worldwide. The main types are cereals, roots, pulses (peas, beans), vegetables, fruits, oil crops, tree nuts, sugar, and spices.
- *Forage crops* such as grass and clover, are grown to feed livestock. Forage crops cover a greater area of the world than food crops.
- *Fibre crops* produce vegetable fibres. Temperate areas produce flax and hemp, but the most valuable fibre crops are cotton, jute, and sisal, which are grown mostly in the tropics.
- *Miscellaneous crops* include tobacco, rubber, ornamental flowers, and plants that produce perfumes, pharmaceuticals, and dyes.

---

**See also**: *agriculture, crop rotation.*

## crop rotation

System of growing different crops, in a particular order, on a piece of land. This method uses, and adds to, the nutrients in the soil and prevents the build-up of insect and fungal pests. Traditionally, a four-year rotation was used:

- year 1: autumn-sown cereal
- year 2: root crop such as turnips, improves the soil and smothers weeds
- year 3: spring-sown cereal

- year 4: legume, such as peas or beans, to build up nitrate in the soil, and because the roots contain bacteria capable of fixing nitrogen from the air.

  **See also**: *agricultural revolution, catch crop*.

## crust

The outermost part of the structure of Earth, consisting of two distinct parts, oceanic crust and continental crust.

- Oceanic crust is on average about 10 km/6.2 mi thick and consists mostly of basalt. Because of the movements of **plate tectonics**, the oceanic crust is in no place older than about 200 million years. Beneath a layer of surface sediment, the oceanic crust is made up of a layer of **basalt**, followed by a layer of gabbro. The composition of the oceanic crust overall shows a high proportion of silicon and magnesium oxides.

- Continental crust is largely made of granite and is more complex in its structure. The continental crust varies in thickness from about 40 km/25 mi to 70 km/45 mi, being deeper beneath mountain ranges. Parts of the continental crust are over 3 billion years old. The surface layer consists of many kinds of **sedimentary** and **igneous** rocks. Beneath lies a zone of **metamorphic** rocks built on a thick layer of granodiorite. Silicon and aluminium oxides dominate the composition of continental crust, making it less dense than oceanic crust.

## culture

The way of life of a particular society or group of people, including patterns of thought, beliefs, behaviour, customs, traditions, rituals, dress, and language, as well as art, music, and literature. Both the UK and the USA are multicultural, and this is widely regarded as enriching the fabric of their societies. That cultural differences can be emphasized in order to divide a society can be witnessed in such conflicts as the civil war in former Yugoslavia.

## current

The flow in a definite direction of a body of water, air, or heat. **Ocean** currents are fast-flowing currents of seawater generated by the wind or by variations in water density between two areas. They are partly responsible for transferring heat from the Equator to the poles and thereby evening out the global heat imbalance.

## TYPES OF OCEAN CURRENT

- Surface currents are wind-driven and move at around 3–5% of the wind speed. They extend 50–100 m/150–300 ft down from the ocean surface. Surface currents are classified as warm or cold, in general cold currents flow from the poles to the Equator and warm currents flow polewards, away from the Equator.
- Deep circulation currents are driven by the temperature and salinity properties of water masses. They move more slowly than surface currents at speeds of 10–50 km/6–30 mi per year.

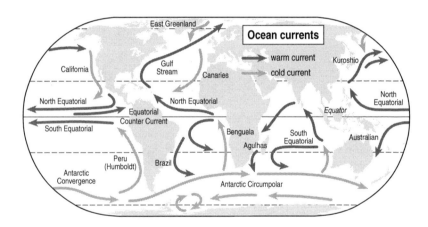

## cyclone

An area of low atmospheric pressure, sometimes called a **depression**. A severe cyclone that forms in the tropics is called a tropical cyclone or **hurricane**.

## dairy farming

The business of rearing cows to produce milk and milk products. Most dairy farms concentrate on the production of milk, while factories deal with its handling, processing, and distribution, as well as the manufacture of dairy products.

---

**FACTS ABOUT DAIRY FARMING**

- In the UK and the USA, over 70% of the milk produced is consumed in its liquid form.
- Areas such as the French Alps and New Zealand rely on easily transportable milk products such as butter, cheese, and condensed and dried milk.
- Overproduction of milk in the European Union has led to the introduction of quotas, which set a limit on the amount of milk for which a farmer may be paid.

---

**See also**: *farming types, livestock, pastoral farming.*

## dam

A barrier built across a river to hold back water in order to prevent flooding, to provide water for irrigation and storage, and to provide hydroelectric power. The biggest dams are of the earth- and rock-fill type. In 1997 there were approximately 40,000 large dams (more than 15 m/45 ft in height) and 800,000 small ones worldwide. Major dams include:

- Rogun (Tajikistan) is the world's highest at 335 m/1,099 ft.
- New Cornelia Tailings (USA) is the world's biggest in volume, 209 million cu m/7.4 billion cu ft.
- Owen Falls (Uganda) has the world's largest reservoir capacity, 204.8 billion cu m/7.2 trillion cu ft.
- Itaipu (Brazil/Paraguay) is the world's most powerful, producing 12,700 megawatts of electricity.

---

**DAMS AND THE ENVIRONMENT**

Although dams can service huge irrigation schemes and are a reliable and cheap source of power, they cause many environmental problems:

- the forcible removal of local communities
- waterlogging and salinization of land
- loss of animals' habitat
- tendency for reservoirs to fill with silt from upstream – which leads to a gradual reduction in reservoir depth and hence in the volume of water held back by the dam - reducing the power delivered by the hydroelectric turbines and harming river and marine life.

---

## death rate

The number of deaths per 1,000 of the population of an area over the period of a year. Death rate is a factor in **demographic transition**. It is lower in wealthier countries; for example, in the USA it is 9/1,000; in Nigeria 18/1,000 because it is linked to social and economic factors such as: standard of living, diet, access to clean water, and availability of medical services.

## debt

Money, goods, or services owed by one person, organization, or country to another.

- The national debt of a country is the total money owed by the government to private individuals, banks, and other financial concerns.
- International debt is the money owed by one country to another, and became a global problem as a result of the oil crisis of the 1970s.

## deciduous

Deciduous trees and shrubs shed their leaves at the end of the growing season or during a dry season to reduce **transpiration**. Oak and beech are deciduous trees. Deciduous trees are often referred to as broad-leaved trees and are the natural vegetation of northern mainland Europe and the British Isles. Many have been felled to make way for farming, industry, and settlement. Broad-leaved trees grow slowly, reaching maturity 100–200 years after being planted, thus limiting their economic value.

**See also**: *afforestation, conifer.*

## deep-sea trench

A deep trench in the seabed indicates the presence of a destructive plate margin, produced by the movements of **plate tectonics**. The subduction or dragging downwards of one plate beneath another means that the ocean floor is pulled down. Ocean trenches are found around the edge of the **Pacific Ocean** and the northeastern **Indian Ocean**; minor trenches occur in the Caribbean and near the Falkland Islands. Deep-sea trenches represent the deepest parts of the ocean floor, the deepest being the Mariana Trench, which has a depth of 11,034 m/36,201 ft.

**See also**: *plate tectonics.*

## deflation

A reduction in the level of economic activity, usually caused by an increase in interest rates and fall in the money supply, increased taxation, or a decline in government expenditure. A government may choose a policy of deflation in order to improve the balance of payments by reducing demand and therefore cutting imports, and lowering inflation to stimulate exports. Deflation can reduce wage increases but may also increase unemployment.

## deforestation

The destruction of forest while neither planting new trees to replace those lost nor working on a cycle that allows the natural forest to regenerate. The wood may be used for timber, fuel, charcoal burning, and the cleared land for agriculture and extractive industries, such as mining. The current wave of deforestation in the tropics dates back only 30 years, but even so has reduced the amount of intact forest ecosystem from 34% of total land in the

**EFFECTS OF DEFORESTATION**

- Deforestation causes fertile soil to be blown away or washed into rivers, leading to **soil erosion, drought, flooding**, and loss of wildlife.
- Reducing the number of trees available to absorb carbon dioxide increases the carbon dioxide content of the atmosphere and intensifies the **greenhouse effect**.
- Great damage is being done to the habitats of plants and animals.
- Deforestation ultimately leads to famine, and is thought to be partially responsible for the flooding of lowland areas – for example, in Bangladesh – because trees help to slow down water movement.

affected areas to 12%. Deforestation in the tropics is especially serious because such forests do not regenerate easily and are a rich source of **bio-diversity**.

**See also**: *afforestation*.

## Countries losing the greatest areas of forest

| Rank | Country | Area of lost forest (hectares) 1990–1995 |
|------|---------|------------------------------------------|
| 1 | Brazil | 2,554,000 |
| 2 | Indonesia | 1,084,000 |
| 3 | Congo, Democratic Republic of | 740,000 |
| 4 | Bolivia | 581,000 |
| 5 | Mexico | 508,000 |
| 6 | Venezuela | 503,000 |
| 7 | Malaysia | 400,000 |
| 8 | Myanmar | 387,000 |
| 9 | Sudan | 353,000 |
| 10 | Thailand | 329,000 |
| 11 | Paraguay | 327,000 |
| 12 | Tanzania | 323,000 |

*Source: State of the World's Forests 1997,* Food and Agriculture Organization of the United Nations.

## degradation

The lowering and flattening of land through **erosion**, especially by **rivers**. Degradation is also used to describe a reduction in the quality of usefulness of environmental resources such as vegetation or soil.

## delta

A triangular-shaped tract of land at a river's mouth, made up of silt deposited as the water slows on entering the sea. Rivers with large deltas include the Mississippi, Ganges and Brahmaputra, Rhône, Po, Danube, and Nile.

- The arcuate delta of the Nile is shaped like the Greek letter delta.

- A birdfoot delta, like that of the Mississippi, is also named because of its shape.

- Tidal deltas, like that of the Mekong, are composed of material that has been swept to one side by sea currents.

## demographic transition

Any change over time in birth and death rates, which may be caused by a variety of social factors (among them education and the changing role of women), and economic factors (such as higher standard of living and improved diet). In some industrialized countries death rate exceeds birth rate, leading to a declining population.

**See also**: *birth rate, death rate.*

## demography

The study of the size, structure, dispersal, and development of human populations used to provide information about birth and death rates, marriages and divorces, life expectancy, and migration. Demography is used by industries and governments to plan and provide education, housing, welfare, transport, and taxation.

## depopulation

The decline of the population of a given area, usually caused by people moving to other areas for economic reasons, rather than an increase in the **death rate** or decrease in **birth rate**.

## deposition

The dropping of material such as soil or rocks when the water, ice, or wind carrying the material slows down. Deposits may also be of organic matter such as plant remains which eventually form coal. They may be eroded again quite quickly, or may remain in place for many millions of years.

**See also**: *erosion, sediment.*

## depression (physical geography)

An area of the Earth's **crust**, such as a basin, which is structurally low due to sinking, down-warping, or downthrusting resulting from tectonic movement.

**See also:** *plate tectonics.*

## Deepest geographical depressions in the world

| Depression | Location | Maximum depth below sea level | |
|---|---|---|---|
| | | m | ft |
| Dead Sea | Israel/Jordan | 400 | 1,312 |
| Turfan Depression | Xinjiang, China | 154 | 505 |
| Lake Assal | Djibouti | 153 | 502 |
| Qattâra Depression | Egypt | 133 | 436 |

## Deepest geographical depressions in the world (*continued*)

| Depression | Location | Maximum depth below sea level | |
|---|---|---|---|
| | | m | ft |
| Poloustrov Mangyshlak | Kazakhstan | 131 | 430 |
| Danakil Depression | Ethiopia | 120 | 394 |
| Death Valley | California, USA | 86 | 282 |
| Salton Sink | California, USA | 71 | 233 |
| Zapadnyy Chink Ustyurta | Kazakhstan | 70 | 230 |
| Priaspiyskaya Nizmennost | Russia/Kazakhstan | 67 | 220 |
| Ozera Sarykamysh | Uzbekistan/Kazakhstan | 45 | 148 |
| El Faiyûm | Egypt | 44 | 144 |
| Valdés Peninsula | Argentina | 40 | 131 |

**depression** (meteorology)
In meteorology, an area of low atmospheric pressure as warm, moist air from the tropics mixes with cold, dry polar air, producing warm and cold fronts and unstable weather such as low cloud and drizzle, showers, or fierce storms. Depressions tend to travel eastwards and can remain active for several days.
**See also**: *cyclone, tornado, typhoon.*

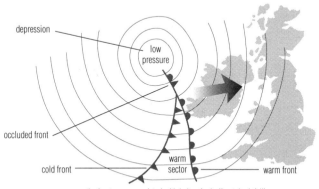

depression label: depression, low pressure, occluded front, cold front, warm sector, warm front

the fronts are associated with belts of rain (frontal rainfall)

**depression** *A typical depression showing low pressure at the centre.*

**desalination**
The removal of salt, usually from sea water, to produce fresh water for irrigation or drinking. This used to be done by distillation, but now polymer

materials that filter the salt from the water are used. Desalination plants are found along the shores of the Middle East where fresh water is in short supply.

## desert

A dry area, with little or no vegetation. Deserts can be either hot or cold and are usually rocky or gravelly, with only a small proportion being covered with sand. Almost 33% of the **Earth's** land surface is desert, and this proportion is increasing.

Characteristics common to all deserts include irregular rainfall of less than 250 mm/19.75 in per year, very high evaporation rates often 20 times the annual precipitation, and low relative humidity and cloud cover. Temperatures are more variable. Tropical deserts have a big diurnal temperature range and very high daytime temperatures (58°C/136.4°F have been recorded at Azizia in Libya). Mid-latitude deserts have a wide annual range and much lower winter temperatures, as in the Mongolian desert, where the mean temperature is below freezing point for half the year. Desert soils are infertile, lacking in **humus**, and generally grey or red in colour.

The few plants capable of surviving desert conditions are widely spaced, scrubby, and often thorny.

- Long-rooted plants (phreatophytes) such as the date palm and musquite commonly grow along dry stream channels.

- Salt-loving plants (halophytes) such as saltbushes grow in areas of highly saline soils and near the edges of dry saline lakes.

- **Xerophytes**, such as succulents and cacti, are drought-resistant and survive by remaining leafless during the dry season or by reducing water losses with small waxy leaves. They frequently have shallow and widely branching root systems and store water during the wet season.

---

### TYPES OF DESERT

- Continental deserts, such as the Gobi, are too far from the sea to receive any moisture.
- Rain-shadow deserts, such as California's Death Valley, lie in the lee of mountain ranges, where the ascending air drops its rain only on the windward slopes.
- Coastal deserts, such as the Namibian, form when cold ocean currents cause local dry air masses to descend.

## Largest deserts in the world

| Desert | Location | Area* | |
|---|---|---|---|
| | | sq km | sq mi |
| Sahara | northern Africa | 9,065,000 | 3,500,000 |
| Gobi | Mongolia/northeastern China | 1,295,000 | 500,000 |
| Patagonian | Argentina | 673,000 | 260,000 |
| Rub al-Khali | southern Arabian peninsula | 647,500 | 250,000 |
| Kalahari | southwestern Africa | 582,800 | 225,000 |
| Chihuahuan | Mexico/southwestern USA | 362,600 | 140,000 |
| Taklimakan | northern China | 362,600 | 140,000 |
| Great Sandy | northwestern Australia | 338,500 | 130,000 |
| Great Victoria | southwestern Australia | 338,500 | 130,000 |
| Kyzyl Kum | Uzbekistan/Kazakhstan | 259,000 | 100,000 |
| Thar | India/Pakistan | 259,000 | 100,000 |

*Desert areas are very approximate because clear physical boundaries may not occur.

**See also**: *desertification.*

## desertification

The natural or human-aided process by which land becomes desert. About 30% of land worldwide is affected by desertification (1998). Desertification can sometimes be reversed by special planting (marram grass, trees) and by

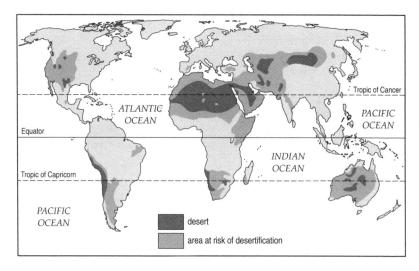

the use of water-absorbent plastic grains, which, when added to the soil, enable crops to be grown. Causes of desertification include:

- **drought**
- increased temperatures
- lowering of the **water table**
- **soil erosion**
- overgrazing
- **deforestation**
- overintensive cultivation.

Pressures of expanding population often lead to desertification, which affects about 135 million people.

### dew
Moisture that collects on the ground and other surfaces during the night. It forms when the ground temperature falls. Air above the ground becomes completely saturated with water vapour evaporated from the soil, which then condenses as small droplets. The temperature at which this happens is called the dew point. Dew can be a very important source of moisture in **arid** areas providing up to 30 mm **precipitation** per year.

### doldrums
The area of low atmospheric pressure along the Equator, where the north-east and southeast trade winds meet. The doldrums are characterized by calm or very light winds, during which there may be sudden squalls and stormy weather. For this reason the areas are avoided as far as possible by sailing ships.

### dormitory town
A town where a high proportion of commuters live and which is at some distance from a centre of work. The original population may have been displaced by these commuters and the settlements enlarged by the building of housing estates.

### drainage
A bog or other wetland may be drained in the process of land **reclamation**, by digging channels draining into a river. A drainage basin is the area drained by a **river** system. The edge of a drainage basin is called the **watershed**.

## drought

A long period when no rain falls. Long droughts cause damage to **agriculture**, deplete the **water table**, and cause famines and disease.

## dry valley

A valley without a river at its bottom, common in **chalk escarpments**. Although dry valleys were probably formed by rivers, the water has now drained away through the permeable chalk. There are two possible reasons for this:

- During a time of **permafrost**, in the last ice age, the chalk might have frozen and been rendered impermeable until the ground eventually thawed.
- Large amounts of meltwater produced at the end of the last ice age might have raised the water table to such a height that rivers could flow and carve out beds without being absorbed by the chalk.

## dune

Mound or ridge of sand, drifted by the wind and common on coasts and in deserts. Loose sand is blown up the windward side of a dune. Sand particles then fall to rest on the leeward side, while more are blown up from the windward side. In this way a dune moves gradually downwind. (*See illustration on opposite page.*)

## dust

Fine particles of solid matter which are moved by the slightest air currents. The dust of the atmosphere consists of tiny fragments of minerals, organic matter, carbon and ash from burning substances, volcanic dust, salt from sea-spray, and dust formed by meteors disintegrating as they enter the atmosphere.

## dust storm

Dust storms occur when large quantities of fine particles are raised into the **atmosphere**,

### FACTS ABOUT DUST

- Air containing water vapour cannot condense unless dust particles are present for the water to condense upon. These minute globules form **cloud, mist, fog** and **rain**.
- Dust creates an explosion risk in some industries, such as sawmills and mines.
- Health can be seriously affected by inhaling dust. Miners are particularly susceptible to disease caused in this way.

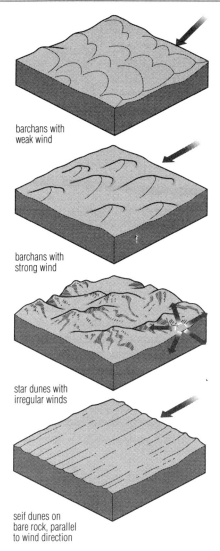

barchans with
weak wind

barchans with
strong wind

star dunes with
irregular winds

seif dunes on
bare rock, parallel
to wind direction

**dune** *The shape of a dune indicates the prevailing wind pattern. Crescent-shaped or barchan dunes form in sandy desert with winds from a constant direction. Seif dunes form on bare rocks, parallel to the wind direction. Irregular star dunes are formed by variable winds.*

reducing visibility to less than 1,000 m/3,280 ft. They happen most often in very dry places. Kuwait International Airport, for example, records an average of 27 dust storms per year.

## Earth

Third most distant planet from the Sun, and the only planet on which life is known to exist. Earth is almost spherical, flattened slightly at the **North** and **South Pole**, and is composed of three concentric layers: the **core**, the **mantle**, and the **crust**. About 70% of the surface is covered with water. The Earth is surrounded by a life-supporting atmosphere. (*See illustration on p. 61.*)

---

**FACTS ABOUT THE EARTH**

**Distance from the Sun**: 149,500,000 km/92,860,000 mi
**Equatorial diameter**: 12,756 km/7,923 mi
**Circumference**: 40,070 km/24,900 mi
**Time taken to rotate**: 23 hr 56 min 4.1 sec
**Time taken to make one complete orbit around the sun**: 365 days 5 hr 48 min 46 sec.
**Average speed around the sun**: 30 kps/18.5 mps
**Land surface**: 150,000,000 sq km/57,500,000 sq mi
**Water surface**: 361,000,000 sq km/139,400,000 sq mi
**Satellite**: the Moon
**Age**: 4.6 billion years. The Earth was formed with the rest of the Solar System by consolidation of interstellar dust. Life began 3.5–4 billion years ago.

---

## earthquake

Abrupt and violent movement of the Earth's surface caused by the sudden release of strain in subterranean rocks. This results from **plate tectonics**. As two plates move past each other they can become jammed. When sufficient strain has accumulated, the rock breaks, releasing a series of waves as the plates spring free. Most earthquakes happen at sea and cause little damage. However, when severe earthquakes occur in highly populated areas they can cause great destruction and loss of life. A reliable form of

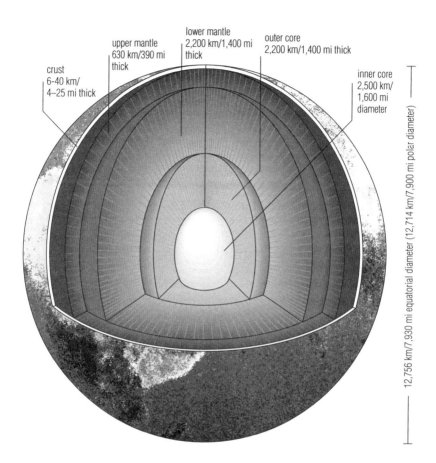

**Earth** *Inside the Earth. The surface of the Earth is a thin crust about 6 km/4 mi thick under the sea and 40 km/25 mi thick under the continents. Under the crust lies the mantle about 2,900 km/1,800 mi thick. The outer core is about 2,200 km/1,400 mi thick, of molten iron and nickel. The inner core is probably solid iron and nickel at a temperature of about 5,000°C/9,000°F.*

earthquake prediction has yet to be developed.

Most earthquakes occur along **faults**. The force of earthquakes is measured on the **Richter scale**. The point at which an earthquake originates is the hypocentre; the point on the Earth's surface directly above this is the epicentre.

---

**NOTABLE EARTHQUAKES**

- The Alaskan earthquake of 27 March 1964 ranks as one of the greatest ever recorded, measuring 8.3 to 8.8 on the Richter scale.
- The 1906 San Francisco earthquake is among the most famous in history. Its magnitude was 8.3 on the Richter scale.
- The deadliest, most destructive earthquake in historical times is thought to have been in China in 1556, and to have killed over 800,000 people.

---

## ecology

Study of the relationship of organisms to each other and to their environments. The chief environmental factors governing the distribution of plants and animals are temperature, humidity, soil, light intensity, hours of daylight, food supply, and interaction with other organisms.

## economy

The set of interconnected activities concerned with the production, distribution, and consumption of goods and services. The contemporary economy is very complex and includes transactions ranging from the distribution and spending of children's pocket money to global-scale financial deals being conducted by **multinational corporations**.

There are several different types of economy, for example:

- a capitalist economy is concerned with individual accumulation of material wealth;
- a socialist economy is concerned with the equal distribution of wealth throughout a community.

## ecosystem

An integrated community of living organisms – bacteria, animals, and plants – and their physical environment – air, soil, water, and climate. Major changes to an ecosystem, such as climate change, overpopulation, or the removal of a species, may threaten the system. For instance, the removal of a major carnivore predator can result in the destruction of an ecosystem through overgrazing by herbivores.

Ecosystems can range from macrosystems to microsystems. The global ecosystem, for instance, consists of all the Earth's physical features – its land, oceans, and enveloping atmosphere – together with all the biological organisms living on Earth. On a smaller scale, a freshwater-pond ecosystem includes the plants and animals living in the pond, the pond water and all the substances dissolved or suspended in that water, together with the rocks, mud, and decaying matter at the bottom of the pond. Thus, ecosystems can contain smaller systems and be contained within larger ones.

The technological revolution of the 20th century, with its programmes of industrialization and urbanization and intensive farming practices, has become a major threat, damaging the planet's ecosystems at all levels.

**See also**: *biodiversity, carrying capacity, food chain, Gaia Hypothesis.*

## ecotourism

Growing trend in tourism to visit sites of ecological interest, for example the Galápagos Islands, or Costa Rica. Ecotourism can generate employment and income for local people, providing an incentive for conservation. However, if carried out unscrupulously it can lead to damage of environmentally sensitive sites.

## El Niño

Warm ocean surge of the Peru Current, which recurs about every 5–8 years in the eastern Pacific off South America. It involves a change in the direction of ocean currents, which prevents the upwelling of cold, nutrient-rich waters along the coast of Ecuador and Peru, and kills fish and plants. It is an important factor in global weather. El Niño usually lasts for about 18 months, but the 1990 occurrence lasted until June 1995; US climatologists estimated this duration to be the longest in 2,000 years.

El Niño is believed to be caused by the failure of trade winds and, consequently, of the ocean currents normally driven by these winds. Warm surface waters then flow in from the east. The phenomenon can disrupt the climate of the area disastrously. El Niño has played a part in causing:

- famine in Indonesia
- drought and bush fires in the Galápagos Islands
- rainstorms in California and South America
- the destruction of Peru's anchovy harvest and wildlife in 1982–83
- the 1997 drought in Australia.

## electoral geography

The study of the geography of elections, including an analysis of the role of **demography** and sociological factors on people's voting behaviour. It also includes the study of how constituency boundaries affect the outcomes of elections.

## emigration and immigration

Immigration is when people move to a country; emigration is when they move from a country, usually their native land. Immigration or emigration on a large scale often happens for economic reasons or because of religious, political, or social persecution (which may create refugees), and often prompts restrictive legislation by individual countries.

The USA has received more than 50 million immigrants during its history.

## energy, alternative

Energy generated from renewable and ecologically safe sources, as opposed to those such as coal, oil, gas, or uranium that are nonrenewable and have toxic by-products. The most important alternative energy source is flowing water, harnessed as **hydroelectricity**. Other sources include:

- the oceans' tides and waves
- **wind power**
- the Sun (solar energy)
- the heat trapped in the Earth's crust (geothermal energy).

## energy consumption

The amount of energy used on Earth continues to rise. Energy is needed to provide heating and lighting and to power industry. As standards of living rise in developing countries, the demand for energy to manufacture goods, supply electricity, for transport, and agriculture will go up. The consumption of oil, for example, has doubled every 12 years during the 20th century. There is a real possibility that 80% of oil reserves will have been used by 2020. World coal resources are sufficient to last for a few more centuries. The rising demand for energy has led both to the development of new ways of extracting fuels, and the search for **alternative energy** sources.

**See also**: *energy resources.*

## energy resources

The natural sources of energy, used for light, heat, and power. The most versatile form of energy is electricity, which can be produced from a wide variety of other energy sources, such as the **fossil fuels – coal, oil**, and **natural gas** – and **nuclear energy** produced from uranium. These are all nonrenewable resources and, in addition, their extraction, transportation, utilization, and waste products all give rise to pollutants of one form or another. The effects of these pollutants can have consequences not only for the local environment, but also at a global level.

---

**FACTS ABOUT ENERGY RESOURCES**

▪ For about 3,000 years, wood, peat, and coal were the main sources of energy. Only in the last 50 years has oil come into significant use and displaced coal as the main fuel source. All these fuels, and natural gas, are known as **fossil fuels**. Burning fossil fuels causes pollution, and is a major cause of **acid rain** and the **greenhouse effect**. Because fossil fuels are nonrenewable and harm the environment, other sources of energy have been developed.

▪ Nuclear energy has developed since the 1940s and now produces about 7% of the world's electricity. The difficulties of safe storage of radioactive waste and the dangers from accidents in nuclear power plants has made the future of nuclear energy uncertain. However, it is still viewed as a viable alternative to fossil fuels if it can be made safer to use.

---

**See also**: *energy, alternative.*

### entrainment
The picking up and carrying of one substance, such as rock particles, by another, such as water, air, or ice. The term is also used in **meteorology**, when one body of air is incorporated into another, for instance, when clear air is entrained into a **cloud**.

### environment
The conditions affecting a particular organism, including physical surroundings, climate, and influences of other living organisms. The term 'the environment' is often used to mean the total global environment, without reference to any particular organism.

Since the Industrial Revolution, the demands made by both the industrialized and developing nations are increasingly affecting the balance of the Earth's resources. Over a period of time, some of these resources are renewable – trees can be replanted, soil nutrients can be replenished – but many resources, such as **fossil fuels** and **minerals**, are nonrenewable and in danger of eventual exhaustion. In addition, humans are creating many other problems which may endanger not only their own survival, but also that of other species, for instance **deforestation**, and **pollution** of air and water.

**See also**: *habitat, global warming, greenhouse effect.*

## environmental impact assessment (EIA)

EIA is the process by which the potential environmental impacts of human activities, such as the construction of a power station, dam, or major housing development, are evaluated. The results of an EIA are published and discussed by different levels of government, non-governmental organizations, and the general public before a decision is made on whether or not the project can proceed.

- Some developments, notably those relating to national defence, are exempt from EIA.
- Increasingly, studies include the impact not only on the physical environment, but also the socio-economic environment, such as the labour market and housing supply.

## environmental lapse rate

The rate at which temperature changes with altitude. Usually, because the **atmosphere** is heated from below, temperatures decrease as altitude increases at an average rate of –6.4°C/–11.5°F per 1,000 m/3,280 ft. The rate varies from place to place and according to the time of day.

Under certain conditions, the lapse rate can be reversed, so that temperatures increase with altitude.

- This can be caused by large scale atmospheric movements, for example where a warm stable air mass overlies a cool, less stable air mass. This is common in trade wind areas of the **Tropics**.
- Smaller scale temperature inversions develop at night where surface temperatures fall rapidly, cooling the air near the surface.
- Cold air may flow down a slope into valleys.

## Equator

The great circle which encircles the broadest part of the Earth, and which represents 0° latitude. The length of the Equator is 40,092 km/24,901.8 mi, divided into 360° longitude. It divides the Earth into two halves, called the northern and the southern hemispheres.

## equinox

The time when the Sun is directly overhead at the **Earth's equator** and consequently day and night are of equal length at all latitudes. This happens twice a year, on 21 March, the spring, or vernal, equinox , and on 23 September, the autumn equinox.

The variation in day lengths occurs because the Earth is tilted on its axis with respect to the Sun. However, because the Earth not only rotates on its own axis, but also orbits the Sun, at the equinoxes the two planets are positioned so that the circle of light from the Sun passes through both of the Earth's poles.

## erosion

The process by which the Earth's surface is worn down, as particles of **rock** and soil are broken down and carried away by the **sea, rivers, glaciers**, and **wind**. People also contribute to erosion by bad farming practices and the cutting down of forests, which can lead to the formation of dust bowls.

There are several processes of erosion:

- **hydraulic action**

- **corrasion**

- **attrition**

- **corrosion**.

Erosion differs from **weathering**, which does not involve transportation of broken down material. **e**

**See also**: *coastal erosion, deforestation.*

## erratic

A rock or boulder that has been transported by a glacier or some other natural force to a site of different geological composition. By tracing erratic rocks back to their source, the course of a glacier can be determined.

## escarpment

Large ridge created by the **erosion** of sedimentary rocks, with one steep side (scarp) and one gently sloping side (dip). Escarpments are common features of chalk landscapes, such as the Chiltern Hills and the North Downs in England. Certain features are associated with chalk escarpments:

- **dry valleys** formed on the dip slope
- combes (steep-sided valleys on the scarp slope)
- **springs**.

### esker
Narrow, steep-walled ridge, often winding and sometimes branching, formed beneath a glacier. An esker is made of sands and gravels, and represents the course of a subglacial river channel. Eskers vary in height from 3–30 m/10–100 ft and can be up to 160 km/100 mi long.

**See also**: *glacier and glaciation.*

### estuary
The point where the mouth of a river widens as it flows into the sea. Fresh water mixes with salt water in an estuary, and the water is tidal. Estuaries can be used as harbours, although may need frequent dredging, as the slowed river currents drop **sediment** which reduces the depth.

### ethical tourism
An approach to **tourism** which seeks to ensure that the local population benefits from tourist development and activities. Although there has been a rapid increase in the number of tourists visiting developing countries, these countries do not always benefit economically. For example, when large international companies build and run tourist resorts, a high percentage of the revenue usually leaves the country and the local economy suffers.

- Ethical tourism promotes the idea that local people should own or be involved in the development of tourism and not simply provide a cheap labour force.
- Ethical tourism may also involve the boycotting of countries with politically repressive regimes.

### ethnic group
A group or society, the members of which feel a common sense of identity, often based on a traditional shared culture, language, religion, and customs. An ethnic group may or may not share common territory, skin colour, or common descent. The USA is often described as a multi-ethnic society because many members would describe themselves as members of an ethnic group (Jewish, black, or Irish, for example) as well as their national group (American).

## Eurasia

The combined land areas of Europe and Asia.

## Europe

The second smallest continent, Europe lies entirely in the northern hemisphere and consists of more than 30 countries, with a combined population in excess of 500 million.

About two-thirds of the continent is a great plain which covers the whole of European Russia and spreads westwards through Poland to the Low Countries and the Bay of Biscay. To the north lie the Scandinavian highlands, to the south, a series of mountain ranges stretch east–west. The Caucasus include Mount Elbrus 5,642 m/18,517 ft, the highest peak in Europe. Mont Blanc 4,807 m/15,772 ft is the highest peak in the Alps. Because of its large number of bays, inlets, and peninsulas, the western coastline is longer in proportion to its size than that of any other continent. There are many rivers over 800 km/500 mi long, including the Volga, Danube, Don, Loire, Rhine, and Rhône. The largest **islands** adjacent to continental Europe include the British Isles, Sicily, and Sardinia.

There are four main climatic zones in Europe:

- The *northwestern region* has mild winters, cool summers, and cloud and rain all the year round with a maximum in the autumn.

- The *Mediterranean zone* has very mild winters, hot, dry summers, and abundant sunshine; with most rain in the spring and autumn.

- In *central Europe* winters are cold and the summers warm, with the maximum rainfall in summer.

- *Eastern Europe* has extremely cold winters.

---

**EUROPEAN INDUSTRIES**

- Nearly 50% of the world's cars are produced in Europe.
- Fertilizer consumption on agricultural land is four times greater than that in any other continent.
- Europe produces 43% of the world's barley, 41% of its rye, 31% of its oats, 24% of its wheat, and more than 70% of its olive oil.

---

Botanically speaking, Europe can be divided into the:

- extreme northern **tundra**

- northern **coniferous** forest
- temperate **deciduous** forest, typified by oak, and beech
- Mediterranean region, rich in plant species, even though much of the evergreen forest has been reduced to dry scrub.

Compared with other continents, Europe has relatively few animal species. Those that remain are characterized by their successful adaptation to life close to humans. They include: deer, badger, fox, rabbits, and squirrels.

## European Union (EU)

Political and economic alliance of 15 European countries, which replaced the European Community in 1993. The original six members – Belgium, France, West Germany, Italy, Luxembourg, and the Netherlands – were joined by the UK, Denmark, and the Republic of Ireland in 1973, Greece in 1981, and Spain and Portugal in 1986. East Germany was incorporated on German reunification in 1990. Austria, Finland, and Sweden joined in 1995. Other countries have also applied to become members. In 1995 there were more than 360 million people living in the EU countries.

The designation European Union was adopted after the signing of the Maastricht Treaty in 1993. The EU embraces not only the various bodies of its predecessor, the EC, but also two intergovernmental 'pillars', covering common foreign and security policy (CFSP) and cooperation on justice and home affairs.

---

**AIMS OF THE EU**

- expansion of trade
- reduction of competition
- abolition of restrictive trading practices
- encouragement of free movement of capital and labour within the alliance
- establishment of a closer union among European people.

---

## eutrophication

Excessive enrichment of **rivers, lakes**, and shallow **seas**, mainly by:

- nitrate fertilizers washed from the soil by **rain**
- phosphates from fertilizers, and from nutrients in municipal sewage
- by sewage itself.

This enrichment encourages the growth of algae and bacteria which use up the oxygen in the water, and make it uninhabitable for fish and other animal life.

## evaporation

Process in which a liquid from a free-standing body of water or saturated surface, turns to a vapour without being boiled. A liquid left to stand in a saucer eventually evaporates because, at any time, a proportion of its molecules will be fast enough to escape through the liquid surface into the **atmosphere**.

The evaporation of liquid water to form water vapour is responsible for the movement of water from the **Earth's** surface to the atmosphere. Evaporation does not include output of water vapour from plants, **evapotranspiration**.

## evapotranspiration

Water lost from vegetated surfaces of the Earth, through transpiration from plants. The difference between actual and potential evapotranspiration is used as a measure of water deficit in an area and is important in water management, for example for irrigation and cropping patterns.

- *Actual evapotranspiration* is the amount that takes place and which is limited by climate and water availability.

- *Potential evapotranspiration* is the amount that could take place assuming particular climatic conditions and unlimited water supply.

## export

The process of producing goods in one country and selling them in another. Exports may be:

- visible, that is goods such as cars which are physically transported

- invisible, that is services such as banking and tourism, that are provided in the exporting country but paid for by residents of another country.

## extinction

The complete disappearance of a species. Extinction occurs when an animal becomes unfit for survival in its natural habitat because the environment has changed, or because the balance of other organisms has altered. For example, a predator's fitness for survival depends upon the availability of its prey.

- Past extinctions: Mass extinctions are episodes during which large numbers of species have become extinct virtually simultaneously, the best known being that of the dinosaurs, other large reptiles, and various marine invertebrates about 65 million years ago. Mass extinctions apparently occur at intervals of approximately 26 million years.

- Current extinctions: A large number of extinctions are attributable to human activity. Some species, such as the dodo of Mauritius, were exterminated by hunting. Others became extinct when their habitat was destroyed. Endangered species are those close to extinction. The rate of extinction is difficult to estimate, but appears to have been accelerated by humans. Conservative estimates put the rate of loss due to **deforestation** alone at 4,000 to 6,000 species a year. Overall, the rate could be as high as one species an hour, with the loss of one species putting those dependent on it at risk.

## factory

A place where goods are made using machinery. The factory system is the basis of manufacturing in the modern world, and the mechanization leads to mass production. In the factory system workers carry out specific tasks, which together result in a product. This is called the division of labour. Richard Arkwright pioneered the system in England in 1771, when he set up a cotton-spinning factory.

**See also**: *industrial revolution.*

## fair trade

A way of conducting international trade so that all parties involved receive fair payments. Fair trade schemes are designed to counteract unjust international trade systems, which often exploit workers in developing countries, by ensuring that all workers are paid a fair price for their skills and products.

## famine

Severe shortage of food affecting a large number of people. Worldwide almost 750 million people (equivalent to double the population of Europe) suffer from hunger and malnutrition. Crop failures do not inevitably lead to famine; nor is it always the case that adequate food supplies are not available nearby. In 1990, for example, the Ethiopian air force bombed grain depots in a rebel-held area. Famines may arise when one group in a society loses its opportunity to exchange its labour or possessions for food.

## farming types

Different approaches to farming, which may be classified:

- according to crop or animal combinations, for example, **arable farming** or **pastoral agriculture**
- according to the dominant product group, for example, **dairy farming** or **market gardening**
- according to the overall approach or techniques used, for example, **organic farming** or **shifting cultivation**.

## fault

A fracture in the **Earth**, on either side of which rocks have moved past one another. Large displacements along a fault are the result of the accumulation of smaller movements (metres or less) over long periods of time. Faults produce features such as block **mountains** and **rift valleys**. Large movements cause detectable **earthquakes**. Faults produce lines of weakness on the Earth's surface that are often exploited by **weathering** and **erosion**. Coastal **caves** and inlets often form along faults and, on a larger scale, rivers may follow the line of a fault.

Faults are planar features. Fault orientation is described by dip, the angle

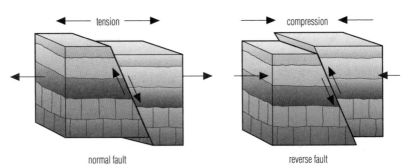

normal fault                                    reverse fault

**fault** *A normal fault occurs where rocks on either side have moved apart, and one block has apparently moved downhill. Reverse faults occur where rocks on either side have been forced together, and one block appears to have moved uphill.*

### TYPES OF FAULT

■ Normal faults occur where one block has apparently moved downhill along a steeply-inclined fault plane.

■ Reverse faults also have fault planes at a high angle, but one block appears to have moved uphill along the fault plane.

■ A thrust fault is reverse fault along a fault plane at a low angle.

■ A lateral fault, or strike-slip fault, occurs where the fault plane is nearly vertical so that the relative movement along the fault plane is sideways.

■ Transform faults give ocean ridges their stepped appearance. The ridge crest is broken into sections, each section offset from the next. Between each section of the ridge crest the newly generated plates are moving past one another, forming a transform fault.

of the fault plane with respect to horizontal, and strike, its orientation with respect to north, south, east, and west.

## fauna
The animal life belonging in any area or period of history, for example, the fauna of Europe, or the fauna of the Antediluvian age.

## fertilizer
Substance containing some or all of a range of about 20 chemical elements necessary for healthy plant growth, used to compensate for the deficiencies of poor or depleted soil. Fertilizers may be:

- organic, for example, farmyard manure, composts, bonemeal, blood, and fishmeal
- inorganic, in the form of compounds, mainly of nitrogen, phosphate, and potash, which have been used on a very much increased scale since 1945.

Fertilizers applied externally often exceed the needs of the plants, and the excess drains away and affects lakes and rivers (**eutrophication**). Research is now directed towards producing beneficial relationships between bacteria and plants, such as legumes, where bacteria in the root nodules fix nitrogen from the atmosphere.

**See also**: *crops, crop rotation.*

## fiord or fjord
Narrow sea inlet enclosed by high cliffs. Fiords are found in Norway, New Zealand, and western parts of Scotland. They are formed when an overdeepened U-shaped **glacial** valley is drowned by a rise in sea level.

## fishing
The harvesting of fish and shellfish from the sea or from freshwater. The world's total fish catch is about 100 million tonnes a year (1995). Fish are an excellent source of protein for humans, and fish products such as oils and bones are used in industry to produce livestock feed, fertilizers, glues, and drugs.

Overfishing has led to serious depletion of stocks, and heated confrontations between countries using the same fishing grounds. A partial solution was the extension of fishing limits to 596 km/370 mi. The North Sea countries have experimented with the artificial breeding of fish eggs and release

---

**TYPES OF FISHING**

■ *Marine fishing*: Most of the world's catch comes from the oceans, and marine fishing accounts for around 20% of the world's animal-based protein. A wide range of species is caught but the majority belong to the herring and cod groups. The majority of the crustaceans landed are shrimp and squid, and bivalves, such as oysters, are dominant among the molluscs.

■ *Freshwater fishing*: Species such as salmon and eels, which migrate to and from fresh and salt water for spawning, may be fished in either system. About one-third of the total freshwater catch comes from fish farming, that is, raising fish (including molluscs and crustaceans) under controlled conditions in tanks and ponds, sometimes in offshore pens. Farmed fish include carp, catfish, trout, Atlantic salmon, turbot, eel, mussels, clams, oysters, and shrimp.

---

of small fry into the sea. New fisheries, such as those for sand eels and queen scallops, have been developed, and new technology, particularly in the field of acoustic fish detection sonar equipment, is now widely used.

## flood
An unusually high discharge from a **river**, which overflows the channel and spills out onto the **flood plain**. Not all floods are catastrophic. The predictable seasonal floods of the Nile allowed the early Egyptian civilization to flourish.

- Long-term flood prediction depends on recording a river's behaviour over a lengthy period and analysing this data statistically.
- Short-term forecasting uses current weather conditions and measurements of ground water to predict specific events.

## flood plain
Low-lying lands adjacent to a **river** which are flooded periodically. As water spills out of the channel, alluvium is deposited on the banks to form levees (raised river banks). This water slowly seeps into the flood plain, depositing a new layer of rich fertile alluvium as it does so. Many important flood plains, such as the inner Niger delta in Mali, occur in **arid** areas where their exceptional productivity has great importance for the local economy.

Flood-control techniques, such as building dams, dredging, and channel modification sometimes fail, and siting towns or villages on flood plains is risky. Flood plains are more suitable for use as parks or agricultural land.

**See also**: *meander, oxbow lakes.*

## flora

All the plants that grow in a particular region, country, or locality, or all the plants of a historical period.

## fog

Cloud formed of water vapour that has condensed on particles of dust in the atmosphere and that collects at ground level. The thickness of fog depends on the number of water particles it contains. When there is a fog, visibility

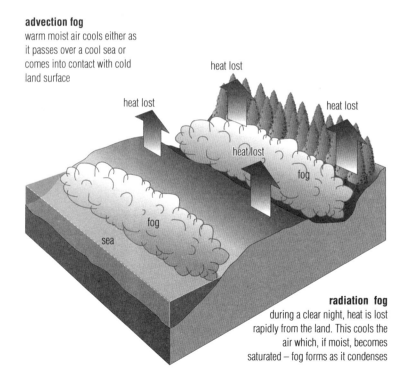

**advection fog**
warm moist air cools either as it passes over a cool sea or comes into contact with cold land surface

heat lost

heat lost

heat lost

heat lost

fog

fog

sea

**radiation fog**
during a clear night, heat is lost rapidly from the land. This cools the air which, if moist, becomes saturated – fog forms as it condenses

**fog** *How advection and radiation fogs are formed.*

is reduced to 1 km/0.6 mi or less. When there is a **mist**, visibility falls to 1–2 km or about 1 mi. In drought areas, such as the Canary Islands or Cape Verde Islands, coastal fogs enable plant and animal life to survive without rain and are a potential source of water for human use.

There are two types of fog:

- An advection fog forms when two currents of air meet, one cooler than the other, or when warm air flows over a cold surface. Sea fogs usually occur where warm and cold currents meet and the air above them mixes.

- A radiation fog forms on clear, calm nights when the land surface loses heat rapidly by radiation; the air above is cooled to below its **dew** point and **condensation** takes place.

## fold mountain

Mountains formed when compression makes rock strata buckle. Over time, this folding can take on very complex forms, and this can sometimes be seen in the rock layers of cliff faces or deep cuttings in the rock. Folding contributed to the formation of great mountain chains such as the Himalayas.

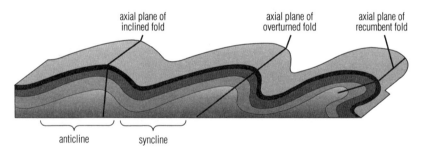

**fold mountain** *Types of folding in fold mountains.*

## food chain

The sequence of feeding relationships between organisms in a particular ecosystem. Each organism depends on the next lowest member of the chain for its food.

Environmentalists have used the concept of the food chain to show how poisons and other forms of pollution can pass from one animal to another,

**HOW THE FOOD CHAIN WORKS**

Energy in the form of food is transferred from producers, principally plants and micro-organisms, to a series of consumers.

The consumers include:

■ herbivores, which feed on the producers
■ carnivores, which feed on the herbivores
■ decomposers, which break down the dead bodies and waste products of all four groups (including their own), ready for recycling.

threatening rare species. For example, the pesticide DDT has been found in lethal concentrations in the bodies of animals at the top of the food chain, such as the golden eagle.

## food supply

The availability of food, usually for human consumption. Food supply can be studied at scales ranging from individual households to global patterns.

• Since the 1940s the industrial and agricultural aspects of food supply have become increasingly globalized.

• New farming, packaging, and distribution techniques mean that the seasonal aspect of food supply has been reduced in wealthier nations such as the USA and UK.

• In some less developed countries there are often problems of food scarcity and distribution caused by climate-related crop failure.

## forest

Area covered by trees which have grown naturally for centuries, instead of being logged at maturity (about 150–200 years). The branches and leaves of a forest, called the canopy, have a range of heights from young and very old trees. Fallen trees also contribute to the very complex **ecosystem**, which may support more than 150 species of mammals and many thousands of species of insects. Globally, forest is estimated to have covered around 68 million sq km/26.25 million sq mi during prehistoric times. By the late 1990s this is believed to have been reduced by half to 34.1 million sq km/13.2 million sq mi.

**See also**: *afforestation, conifer, deforestation, forestry.*

## forestry

The science and practice of forest management, which aims to fulfil several purposes, including the preservation of varied plant and animal species, and the provision of trees for use as timber. Forestry has often been confined to the planting of a single species, such as a rapid-growing conifer providing softwood for paper pulp and construction timber, for which world demand is greatest. In tropical countries, logging contributes to the destruction of **rainforests**, causing global environmental problems.

**See also**: *deforestation*.

## fossil

An internal cast, external impression, or the actual remains of an animal or plant preserved in rock. Fossils were created when rocks were formed over millions of years by the gradual accumulation of sediment at the bottom of the sea bed or an inland **lake**. A few fossils are preserved intact, as with mammoths fossilized in Siberian ice, or insects trapped in tree resin that is today amber. About 250,000 fossil species have been discovered.

## fossil fuel

Fuel, such as **coal, oil**, and **natural gas**, formed from the fossilized remains of plants that lived hundreds of millions of years ago. Fossil fuels are a nonrenewable **energy resource** and will eventually run out. Extraction of coal and oil causes considerable environmental **pollution**, and burning coal contributes to problems of **acid rain** and the **greenhouse effect**.

## front

The boundary between two air masses of different temperature or humidity. Frontal systems define the weather of the mid-latitudes, where warm tropical air is constantly meeting cold air from the poles. Warm air, being lighter, tends to rise above the cold; its moisture is carried upwards and usually falls as rain or snow, hence the changeable weather conditions at fronts.

- A *cold front* marks the line of advance of a cold air mass from below, as it displaces a warm air mass.

- A *warm front* marks the advance of a warm air mass as it rises up over a cold one.

- An *occluded front* occurs where a cold front catches up with a warm front and merges with it.

  **See also**: *depression*.

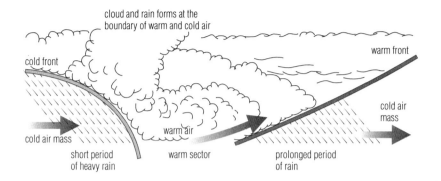

cloud and rain forms at the
boundary of warm and cold air

warm front

cold front

cold air
mass

warm air

cold air mass

short period
of heavy rain

warm sector

prolonged period
of rain

**front** *The boundaries between two air masses of different temperature and
humidity. A warm front is when warm air displaces cold air. If cold air
replaces warm air, it is called a cold front.*

## frost

Frozen dew that forms when the air temperature is below freezing,
0°C/32°F. Water in the atmosphere is deposited as ice crystals on the
ground or exposed objects. Because cold air is heavier than warm, ground
frost is more common than hoar frost, which clings to walls and windows.

## Gaia hypothesis
Theory that the Earth's living and nonliving systems form an inseparable whole that is regulated by living organisms themselves. The planet therefore functions as a huge single organism, or a giant cell. The hypothesis was put forward by British scientist James Lovelock in 1968.

> ❝ When I first introduced Gaia, I had vague hopes that it might be denounced from the pulpit and thus made acceptable to my scientific colleagues. As it was, Gaia was embraced by theologians and by a wide range of New Age writers and thinkers, but denounced by biologists. ❞
>
> **James Lovelock**, quoted in *Earthwatch*, 1992

## gentrification
The movement of higher social or economic groups into an area after it has been renovated and restored. This may result in the outmigration of the people who previously occupied the area. Classifying an area as a conservation area encourages gentrification. It is one strategy available to planners in **urban** renewal schemes within the inner city.

## geography
The study of the **Earth's** surface; its **topography, climate**, and physical conditions, and how these factors affect people and society.

- *Physical geography* deals with the natural physical attributes of the Earth's surface. It includes the study of processes and landforms as well as how these are related to the distribution of **flora** and **fauna**, **weather**, climate, etc. Sub-types include biogeography, geomorphology, **meteorology**.

- *Human geography* is concerned with the role and activities of humans, and their relation to the physical environment. It includes the study of patterns of economic and social development and of the ways in which people use and are affected by the places in which they live. Sub-types include cultural, social, economic and political geography.

The foundation of modern geography as an academic subject stems from the writings of Friedrich Humboldt and Johann Ritter, in the late 18th and early 19th centuries. They defined geography as a major branch of scientific inquiry for the first time.

## geology

Science of the **Earth's**, origin, composition, structure, and history. It is divided into several branches:

- mineralogy, the minerals of Earth
- petrology, the origin of rocks
- stratigraphy, the deposition of successive beds of sedimentary rocks
- palaeontology, fossils
- tectonics, the deformation and movement of the Earth's crust.

Geology is regarded as part of earth science, a more widely embracing subject that brings in meteorology, oceanography, geophysics, and geochemistry.

## geyser

Natural spring that intermittently discharges an explosive column of steam and hot water into the air due to the build-up of steam in underground chambers. One of the most remarkable geysers is Old Faithful, in Yellowstone National Park, Wyoming, USA. Geysers also occur in New Zealand and Iceland.

## glacier and glaciation

A glacier is a tongue of ice, which moves slowly down a mountain and is constantly replenished from its source. When a glacier moves over an uneven surface, deep **crevasses** are formed in the rigid upper layers of the ice mass. The most extensive period of recent glacial **erosion** was about 18,000 years ago, when ice sheets covered most of Europe, North America, and Asia.

Glaciers form where annual snowfall exceeds annual melting and drainage. The area at the top of the glacier is called the zone of accumulation. The lower area of the glacier is called the zone of **ablation**. In the zone of accumulation, the snow compacts to ice under the weight of the layers above and moves downhill under the force of gravity. The ice moves plastically under pressure, changing its shape and crystalline structure permanently. The underside of the glacier, where it contacts the bedrock is called the sole of the glacier. Partial melting of ice at the sole also produces a sliding component of glacial movement, as the ice travels over the bedrock. In the ablation zone, melting occurs and glacial moraine is deposited.

Erosion, caused as a glacier moves across the surface of the land, and deposition, caused as rocky material is dropped when the ice melts, produce the characteristic geographical features of a glaciated landscape.

---

**FEATURES OF GLACIATION**

- glacial troughs or U-shaped valleys, associated with truncated spurs, the ends of which have been sheared away by ice, and hanging valleys that enter the trough at a higher level than the trough floor.
- **corries**
- **arêtes**
- **eskers**
- **moraines**
- drumlins, egg-shaped hills
- **ribbon lakes**
- cirques, steep-sided, flat-floored valleys
- **erratics**.

---

## global positioning system (GPS)

US satellite-based navigation system, comprising a network of 24 satellites in six orbits, each circling the **Earth** once every 24 hours. Each satellite sends out a continuous time signal, plus an identifying signal. To fix position, a user needs to be within range of four satellites, one to provide a reference signal and three to provide directional bearings. The user's receiver can then calculate the position from the difference in time between receiving the signals from each satellite.

## global warming

An increase in average global temperature of approximately 1°F/0.5°C over the past century. This coincides with the spread of industralization, prompting the theory that it is the result of an accelerated **greenhouse effect** caused by atmospheric pollutants, especially carbon dioxide gas. However, natural climatic variations have not been ruled out as the cause of the current global rise in temperature. Melting of ice is expected to raise sea levels in the coming decades.

---

### CHRONOLOGY OF GLOBAL WARMING

**1967**  US scientists warn that an increase in carbon dioxide in **atmosphere** will raise temperatures and cause sea levels to rise.

**1968**  A 10-year programme is launched to study and predict climate change.

**1969**  Warmest year on record worldwide.

**1970**  Convention signed to combat global warming.

**1971**  Larsen Ice Shelf in Antarctica beings to disintegrate.

**1997**  Conference in Kyoto, Japan, agrees to cut emissions of greenhouse gases by 5.2% from 1990 levels by 2012.

**1998**  Warmest year on record, with average global temperature of 14.4°C/ 58°F.

---

## globalization

The process by which different parts of the globe become interconnected by economic, social, cultural, and political means, or through natural phenomena. Globalization has become increasingly rapid over the last 30 years. **Global warming** and the international operation of financial markets are examples of processes operating on a global scale.

## gneiss

Coarse-grained **metamorphic rock** formed under conditions of high temperature and pressure, and often occurring in association with schists (rock in which the various minerals have crystallized into thin layers) and **granites**. Gneisses are formed during regional metamorphism. They have a layered structure consisting of thin bands of dark and light minerals.

- Paragneisses are derived from metamorphism of **sedimentary rock**.
- Orthogneisses are derived from metamorphism of **granite** or similar **igneous rock**.

## gorge
Narrow steep-sided **valley** or **canyon** that may or may not have a river at the bottom. A gorge may be formed as a **waterfall** retreats upstream, eroding the rock at the base of a river valley; or it may be caused when a river begins to cut downwards into its channel once again, for example, in response to a fall in sea level. Gorges are common in limestone country, where they may be formed by the collapse of the roofs of underground caves.

## gradient
The rate at which a piece of land slopes over a certain horizontal distance. Gradient may be expressed:

- in simple terms – flat, gentle, or steep
- numerically, as a percentage of horizontal distance
- as a fraction, vertical distance over horizontal distance.

## granite
Coarse-grained **igneous** rock, typically consisting of the quartz, feldspar, and mica, and chiefly used as a building material. Granite may be pink or grey, depending on the composition of the feldspar. Granites often form large intrusions in the core of **mountain** ranges, and have characteristic **moorland** scenery.
    **See also**: *tor.*

## grassland
Area covered with wild grass, called prairies in North America and steppes in central Asia. Large areas of the world are covered by grassland. (*See map on opposite page.*)

## green belt
Area surrounding a large city, which must not be built on but preserved as open space for agricultural and recreational use. In the UK the first green belts were established from 1938 around **conurbations**, such as London, in order to prevent urban sprawl. New towns were set up to take the overspill population.

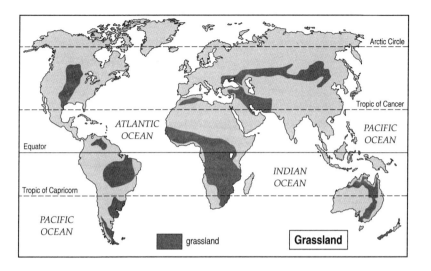

grassland

**Grassland**

## greenhouse effect

Process by which solar radiation, trapped by the Earth and re-emitted from the surface as infrared radiation, is prevented from escaping by various gases in the air. The result is **global warming**. The main greenhouse gases are carbon dioxide, methane, and **CFCs**, as well as water vapour. **Fossil-fuel** consumption and forest fires are the principal causes of carbon dioxide build-up. The United Nations Environment Programme estimates that by 2025, average world temperatures will have risen by 1.5°C/2.7°F with a consequent rise of 20 cm/7.9 in in sea level. Low-lying areas and entire countries would be threatened by flooding and crops would be affected by the change in climate. However, predictions about global warming and its possible climatic effects are tentative and often conflict with each other.

At the 1992 Earth Summit it was agreed that by 2000 countries would stabilize carbon dioxide emissions at 1990 levels, but to halt the acceleration of global warming, emissions would probably need to be cut by 60%. (*See illustration on p. 88.*)

**See also**: *acid rain, global warming.*

## green revolution

The change in arable farming methods instigated in the 1940s and 1950s in Third World countries, with the aim of providing more and better food for their populations, albeit with a heavy reliance on chemicals and machinery. The green revolution was abandoned by some countries in the 1980s.

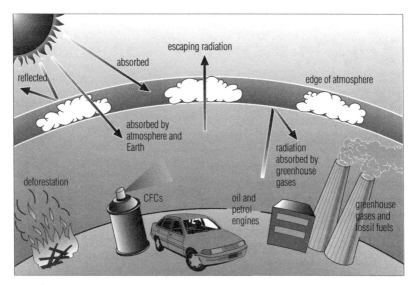

**greenhouse effect** *The greenhouse effect occurs as radiation from the Sun enters the atmosphere but is prevented from escaping back into space by gases that build up in the atmosphere. As this process continues, the Earth's average temperature is expected to rise.*

Much of the food produced was exported as **cash crops**, so that local diet did not always improve.

In terms of production, the green revolution was initially successful in southeast Asia; India doubled its wheat yield in 15 years, and the rice yield in the Philippines rose by 75%. However, yields have levelled off in many areas; and some countries that cannot afford the dams, fertilizers, and machinery required, have adopted intermediate technologies.

### Greenwich Meridian
The zero line of longitude, which passes through the Old Royal Observatory at Greenwich, London. Although the term Greenwich Mean Time (GMT), meaning the average solar time on the Meridian, is still widely used, the time-scale was replaced in 1986 by coordinated universal time (UTC). The Meridian continues to be used to measure longitudes and the world's standard time zones.

### grid reference
A numbering system used to specify location on a map. The numbers representing grid lines at the bottom of the map (eastings) are given before

those at the side (northings). On British Ordnance Survey maps, a four-figure grid reference indicates a specific square, whereas a six-figure grid reference indicates a point within a square.

### gross domestic product (GDP)
Value of all goods and services produced within a nation's borders, normally given as a total for the year. It includes the production of foreign-owned firms located within the country, but excludes the income from domestically owned firms located abroad. In some countires the percentage increase in GDP from one year to the next is the standard measure of economic growth.

**See also**: *gross national product.*

### gross national product (GNP)
The most commonly used measurement of the wealth of a country, defined as the total value of all goods and services produced by firms owned by the

## Countries with the highest GNP per head

| Country | GNP per head (US $)* |
|---|---|
| Switzerland | 35,500 |
| Japan | 32,018 |
| Luxembourg | 31,080 |
| Sweden | 29,600 |
| Denmark | 28,200 |
| Norway | 28,200 |
| Finland | 24,400 |
| Belgium | 22,600 |
| Iceland | 22,580 |
| USA | 22,520 |
| Canada | 21,170 |
| Netherlands | 21,400 |
| Liechtenstein | 21,020 |
| Italy | 20,200 |
| United Arab Emirates | 19,680 |
| Singapore | 18,143 |
| Australia | 17,320 |
| UK | 17,300 |

*Based on 1990–92 estimates.

## Countries with the lowest GNP per head

| Country | GNP per head (US $)* |
|---|---|
| Mozambique | 80 |
| Ethiopia | 120 |
| Tanzania | 120 |
| Somalia | 150 |
| Nepal | 170 |
| Guinea-Bissau | 180 |
| Chad | 190 |
| Bhutan | 190 |

*Based on 1990–92 estimates.

country concerned. It is measured as the **gross domestic product** plus income from abroad, minus income earned during the same period by foreign investors within the country.

## groundwater
Water collected underground in porous rock strata and soils which emerges at the surface as springs and streams. The groundwater's upper level is called the **water table**. Rock beds filled with groundwater are called **aquifers**. Recent estimates are that usable ground water amounts to more than 90% of all the fresh water on Earth. However, keeping such supplies free of pollutants is a critical environmental concern.

## groyne
Wooden or concrete barrier built at right angles to a **beach** in order to prevent the movement of material along the beach by **longshore drift**. Groynes are usually successful in protecting individual beaches, but because they prevent material from passing along the coast their use can deprive other beaches of sand and shingle, placing them in danger of being eroded by waves.

**See also**: *coastal erosion.*

## Gulf Stream
Warm ocean current that flows north from the warm waters of the Gulf of Mexico along the east coast of America, from which it is separated by a channel of cold water originating in the southerly Labrador current. Off Newfoundland, part of the current is diverted east across the Atlantic, where it is known as the North Atlantic Drift, dividing to flow north and south, and warming what would otherwise be a colder climate in the British Isles and northwest Europe. At its beginning, the temperature of the Gulf Stream is about 26°C/79°F. As it flows northwards, the current cools and becomes broader and less rapid.

**See also**: *Atlantic Ocean, current, ocean.*

## gully
A long, narrow, steep-sided valley with a flat floor. Gullies are formed by water erosion and are more common in unconsolidated rock and soils that are easily eroded. They may be formed very rapidly during periods of heavy rainfall and are common in arid areas that have periods of heavy rain. Gully formation in more temperate areas is common where the **vegetation** cover

has been destroyed or reduced, for example as a result of fire or agricultural clearance.

## gust

A temporary increase in **wind** speed, lasting less than two minutes. Gusts are caused by rapidly moving air in higher layers of the **atmosphere**, mixing with slower air nearer the ground. Gusts are common in **urban** areas, where winds are funnelled between closely spaced high buildings. Gusting winds do far more damage to buildings and crops than steady winds. The strongest gusts can exceed speeds of 100 m/328 ft per second.

## guyot

A flat-topped volcanic mountain on the ocean bed. Also known as a tablemount, guyots are **seamounts** whose tops have suffered extensive erosion.

## habitat
Environment in which organisms live, and which provides for all, or almost all, of their needs. The diversity of habitats found within the **Earth's ecosystem** is enormous, and they are changing all the time. Many habitats are physical features; for example, the **arctic** ice **cap**, a **cave**, or a cliff face. Others are more complex; for instance, a woodland or a **forest** floor. Some habitats are so precise that they are called microhabitats, such as the area under a stone where a particular type of insect lives.

## hail
Pellets of ice, or hailstones, that fall from the **atmosphere**. Water droplets freeze as they are carried upwards by strong convection currents, usually within cumulonimbus **clouds**. As the circulation continues, layers of ice are deposited around the droplets until they become too heavy to be supported by the currents and they fall as a hailstorm.

Hailstones can kill. In the Gopalganji region of Bangladesh, in 1988, 92 people died after being struck by huge hailstones weighing up to 1 kg/2.2 lb.

## hamlet
Small rural settlement that is more than just an isolated dwelling but not large enough to be termed a **village**. Typically it has a population of between 11–100 people.

## headland
An area of land running out into the sea. Headlands are often high points on the coastline and may be made of more resistant rock than that in adjacent bays.
  **See also**: *coastal erosion.*

## hemisphere
Half of the globe's sphere. The **Equator** divides the planet **Earth** into the northern and southern hemispheres.

## hot spot
An isolated rising plume of molten **mantle** material that may rise to the surface of the Earth's crust creating features such as volcanoes, chains of ocean islands, and **seamounts**. Hot spots are responsible for large amounts of volcanic activity within tectonic plates rather than at plate margins.

Chains of volcanic seamounts trace the movements of tectonic plates as they pass over hot spots. Immediately above a hot spot on the oceanic crust a volcano will form. This volcano is then carried away by plate tectonic movement, and becomes extinct. A new volcano forms beside it, again above the hot spot. The result is an active volcano and a chain of increasingly old and eroded extinct volcanoes stretching away along the line traced by the plate movement. The chain of volcanoes comprising the Hawaiian Islands and Emperor Seamount chain formed in this way.

Volcanism from a hot spot also forms the unique features of Yellowstone National Park, Wyoming, USA, and the same hot spot that built Iceland atop the **Mid-Atlantic ridge** in the North Atlantic Ocean also produced the voluminous volcanic rocks of the Isle of Skye in Scotland.

## humidity
The amount of moisture present in the **atmosphere**. It may be measured as:

- absolute humidity, the quantity of water vapour present in a given volume of the atmosphere
- specific humidity, the ratio of the mass of water vapour in the air to the combined mass of the water vapour and the air
- relative humidity, the ratio of the amount of water vapour in the atmosphere to the saturation value at the same temperature. At **dew** point the relative humidity is 100% and the air is said to be saturated, that is, containing the maximum amount of water vapour possible.

## humus
Dark-coloured decomposed or partly decomposed organic matter, found in **soil**. Humus is usually richer towards the surface. It has a higher carbon content than the original material and a lower nitrogen content and is an important source of minerals in soil fertility.

## hunting and gathering
A way of supporting human life by hunting animals and gathering seeds, nuts, roots, and berries. Hunting and gathering was the main means of subsistence for 99% of human history. With the development of agriculture

and animal domestication in the Neolithic period (from 9000 BC), hunting and gathering gradually declined in importance. The Australian Aborigines, Inuit, Kung, and Pygmies are among the few remaining peoples who live chiefly by hunting and gathering.

## hurricane

A severe revolving storm in tropical regions, accompanied by lightning and torrential rain, which can cause extensive damage. A central calm area, called the eye, is surrounded by inwardly spiralling winds of up to 320 kph/200 mph. A hurricane can also be a wind of force 12 or more on the Beaufort scale.

### Worst hurricanes of the 20th century

| Year | Date | Location | Deaths |
|------|------|----------|--------|
| 1900 | Aug–Sept | Galveston, Texas | 6,000 |
| 1926 | 20 Oct | Cuba | 600 |
| 1928 | 6–20 Sept | Southern Florida | 1,836 |
| 1930 | 3 Sept | Dominican Republic | 2,000 |
| 1938 | 21 Sept | Long Island, New York, New England | 600 |
| 1942 | 15–16 Oct | Bengal, India | 40,000 |
| 1963 | 4–8 Oct | (Flora) Caribbean | 6,000 |
| 1974 | 19–20 Sept | (Fifi) Honduras | 2,000 |
| 1979 | 30 Aug–7 Sept | (David) Caribbean, eastern USA | 1,100 |
| 1989 | 16–22 Sept | (Hugo) Caribbean, southeast USA | 504 |

## hydraulic action

Process of **erosion** exerted by water (as distinct from the forces exerted by rocky particles carried by water). Hydraulic action can wear away the banks of a river, particularly at the outer curve of a **meander** where the current flows most strongly. The process also occurs as a river tumbles over a **waterfall** to crash onto the rocks below, which leads to the formation of a plunge pool below the waterfall.

The hydraulic action of ocean waves and turbulent currents causes cavitation by forcing air into rock cracks, exerting great pressure and eventually causing rocks to break apart.

## hydroelectricity

Electricity generated by harnessing the power of moving water. About one-fifth of the world's electricity comes from hydroelectric power. Hydroelectricity is a renewable resource.

## HOW HYDROELECTRICITY IS GENERATED

In a typical scheme, water stored in a reservoir, often created by damming a river, is piped into water turbines, coupled to electricity generators. In pumped storage plants, water flowing through the turbines is recycled. A tidal power station exploits the rise and fall of the tides.

## hydrological cycle

The continuous cycle by which water is circulated between the **Earth's** surface and its **atmosphere**, also known as the water cycle. Around 97% of the water is stored in the oceans. The rest is in **glaciers** and **ice caps**, in **rivers** and **lakes**, and as **groundwater**. Water circulates between the Earth and the atmosphere in several ways.

- Water evaporates from the oceans.
- It is carried by winds until eventually it falls back to earth as **precipitation**.
- If the water falls into the sea, the cycle is completed.
- If it falls on land, it filters through the earth back into rivers or down to stores of groundwater. From here, it will eventually evaporate back into the atmosphere.

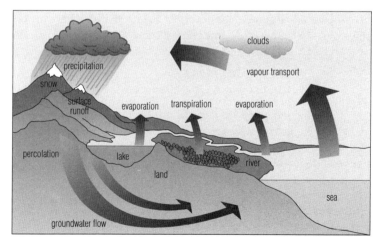

**hydrological cycle** *During the hydrological cycle about 380,000 cubic km/cubic mi of water is evaporated every year. The entire contents of oceans would take one million years to pass through the hydrological cycle.*

### ice age
Any period of **glaciation** occurring in the **Earth's** history, but particularly that in the Pleistocene epoch, which immediately preceded historic times. On the North American continent, glaciers reached as far south as the Great Lakes, and an **ice sheet** spread over northern Europe, leaving its remains as far south as Switzerland. There is a possibility that the Pleistocene ice age is not yet over. It may reach another maximum in another 60,000 years.

### ice cap
A body of ice larger than a **glacier**, but smaller than an **ice sheet**. Such ice masses cover mountain ranges such as the Alps, or small islands. Glaciers often originate from ice caps.

    **See also:** *arctic.*

### iceberg
A floating mass of ice, about 80% of which is submerged, and which can rise to 100 m/300 ft above sea level. A glacier that reaches the coast becomes extended into a broad foot. As this enters the sea, masses break off into icebergs and drift towards temperate latitudes, becoming a danger to shipping.

### ice sheet
A body of ice, larger than an **ice cap**, that covers a large land mass or continent. During the last **ice age**, ice sheets spread over large parts of Europe and North America. Today there are two ice sheets, covering much of Antarctica and Greenland. About 96% of all present-day ice exists in the form of ice sheets.

### igneous rock
Rock formed when molten **magma** or **lava** cools and solidifies, and made largely of silica.

- Intrusive igneous rocks cool slowly from magma below the **Earth's** surface and have large crystals. Examples include dolerite and **granite**.

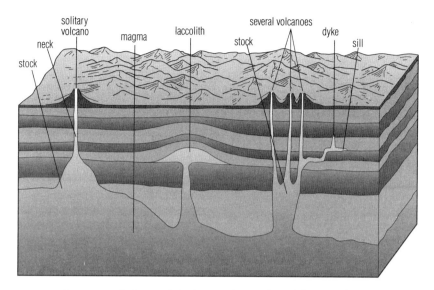

**igneous rock** *Igneous intrusions can be a variety of shapes and sizes. Laccoliths are domed circular shapes, and can be many miles across. Sills are intrusions that flow between rock layers. Pipes or necks connect the underlying magma chamber to surface volcanoes*

- Igneous rocks extruded at the surface from lava cool rapidly and so form small crystals. These are called extrusive. **Basalt** is an example.

## immigration
See *emigration and immigration.*

## imperialism
See *colonialism.*

## import
Product or service that one country purchases from another for domestic consumption, or for processing and re-exporting. Imports may be visible (goods) or invisible (services). If an importing country does not have a counterbalancing value of exports, it may experience balance-of-payments difficulties and restrict imports by imposing tariffs or quotas.

## Indian Ocean
The Indian Ocean lies between Africa and Australia, with India to the north, and the southern boundary being an arbitrary line from Cape Agulhas to

south Tasmania. With an area of 73,500,000 sq km/28,371,000 sq mi, it includes two great bays on either side of the Indian peninsula, the Bay of Bengal to the east, and the Arabian Sea. The Indian Ocean also includes the gulfs of Aden and Oman to the west.

- *Depth* The ocean's average depth is 3,872 m/12,708 ft, the greatest depth being the Java Trench, which is 7,725 m/25,353 ft deep.

- *Islands* The many islands include those of coral formation such as the Maldives, the Chagos Archipelago, and the Cocos. Others are volcanic, such as Crozet and St Paul's islands. The chief islands in the west are Madagascar, Mauritius, Bourbon, the Seychelles, and Socotra, while the main ones in the east are the Laccadives, the Maldives, Sri Lanka, and the Andaman and Nicobar islands.

- *Rivers* The main rivers flowing into the Indian Ocean are the Zambezi, Indus, Ganges, Brahmaputra, Irrawaddy, Godavari, and Krishna.

- *Straits* There are two important straits, the Mozambique Channel in the west, separating Africa from Madagascar, and Palk Strait in the east, separating India from Sri Lanka.

- *Currents* The Mozambique and Agulhas currents are warm and move southwards; in the east, the colder Western Australian current crosses the Indian Ocean moving northwards. North of the equator the currents vary with the monsoon. From November to March, there are northeast winds and the current flows from India towards Africa. From May to September, southwest winds reverse the current to flow from Africa towards India. This is the only example of an annual reversal of direction by a large oceanic current.

## industrial revolution

The sudden acceleration of technical and economic development that began in Britain in the second half of the 18th century, and replaced the traditional agricultural economy with one dominated by machinery and manufacturing. This transferred the balance of political power from the landowner to the industrial capitalist and created an urban working class. The process of industrialization was long drawn out, erratic, and varied from industry to industry and from country to country. From 1830 to the early 20th century, the industrial revolution spread throughout Europe and the USA and to Japan and the various colonial empires.

---

**MAJOR EVENTS OF THE INDUSTRIAL REVOLUTION**

- Use of new materials such as iron and steel, new energy sources, such as coal and the steam engine, and new machinery, particularly in the textile industry.
- Transport systems were revolutionized by steam trains, canals, and better roads.
- Cottage industries were replaced by **factories**, involving new methods of labour organization.
- Massive social changes brought about by internal migration, a rising population, and the growth of urban areas.
- Political reforms were designed to give growing industrial centres proper representation and extend the right to vote.

## industry

The extraction and conversion of raw materials, the manufacture of goods, and the provision of services. Industry can be:

- low technology, unspecialized, and labour-intensive, as in countries with a large unskilled labour force
- highly automated, mechanized, and specialized, using advanced technology, as in the industrialized countries.

Major recent trends in industrial activity have been the growth of electronic, robotic, and microelectronic technologies, the expansion of the offshore oil industry, and the prominence of Japan and other Pacific-region countries in manufacturing and distributing electronics, computers, and motor vehicles. In British industry the last 30 years have seen the growth of the offshore oil and gas industries, the rapid expansion of electronic and microelectronic technologies, and a continuous rise in the share of total employment of service industries. At the same time there has been a decline in traditional industries, such as steel-making, ship-building, and coal mining.

## infant mortality rate

The number of infants dying under the age of one year, usually expressed as the number of deaths per 1,000 live births. Improved sanitation, nutrition, and medical care have considerably lowered figures throughout much of the world. For example, in the 18th century in the UK infant mortality was about 500 per thousand compared with under 10 per thousand in

1989. The lowest infant mortality rate is in Japan, at 4.5 per 1,000 live births. In much of the Third World however, infant mortality remains high.

## infiltration

The absorption of water into the soil. Once in the soil, water may pass into the bedrock to form **groundwater**. The rate of absorption of surface water by soil (the infiltration capacity) depends on:

- the intensity of rainfall
- the permeability and compactness of the soil
- the extent to which the soil is already saturated with water.

## infrastructure

The services that enable an industrialized country to function efficiently. Infrastructure usually includes roads, railways, other communication networks, energy and water supply, and education and training facilities. It may also include health-care and leisure facilities.

## inlet

A narrow strip of sea water penetrating into the land.
    **See also**: *estuary, fault, fiord.*

## inselberg

Prominent steep-sided hill of rock such as **granite**, rising out of a plain, usually in a tropical area. Its rounded appearance is caused by so-called onion-skin **weathering**, in which the surface is eroded in successive layers. The Sugar Loaf in Rio de Janeiro harbour in Brazil, and Ayers Rock in Northern Territory, Australia, are famous examples.

## interception

Process by which trees and plants hinder the passage of rain on its way to the ground. High rates of interception slow down the transfer of rainwater into rivers and make **flooding** less likely.

## International Date Line (IDL)

Imaginary line that approximately follows the 180° meridian of longitude. The line crosses very little land, as it passes mainly across the waters of the **Pacific Ocean**. When a ship or aircraft crosses the line heading west, the date is put forward one day. When crossing to the east, the date goes back by one day.

## Internet

Global computer network connecting governments, companies, universities, and many other networks and users, including millions of private individuals.

---

**THE GROWTH OF THE INTERNET**

■ The Internet began in the mid-1980s with funding from the US National Science Foundation as a means to allow US universities to share the resources of five regional supercomputing centres.

■ The number of users grew quickly, and in the early 1990s access became cheap enough for domestic users to have their own links on home personal computers.

■ Electronic mail, electronic conferencing, educational and chat services are all supported across the network, as is the ability to access remote computers and send and retrieve files.

■ In 1997 around 60 million adults had access to the Internet in the USA alone.

■ In 1998 the Internet generated $301 billion in revenue, and created 1.2 million jobs.

---

## irrigation

Method of providing a water supply to dry agricultural areas using dams and channels. Drawbacks of irrigation are that it tends to concentrate salts at the surface, ultimately causing soil infertility, and that rich river silt is retained at dams, to the impoverishment of the land and fisheries below them.

**See also**: *dam*.

## island

Area of land surrounded entirely by water. Islands can be formed in many ways.

- **Continental islands** were once part of the mainland, but became isolated by, for example, tectonic movement, **erosion**, or a rise in sea level.

- **Volcanic islands**, such as Japan, were formed by underwater volcanoes.

- **Coral islands** consist mainly of **coral**, built up over many years.

- **Barrier islands** are found by the shore in shallow water, and are formed by the deposition of sediment eroded from the shoreline.

## The ten largest islands in the world

| Island | Location | Area | |
|---|---|---|---|
| | | sq km | sq mi |
| Greenland | northern Atlantic | 2,175,600 | 840,000 |
| New Guinea | southwestern Pacific | 800,000 | 309,000 |
| Borneo | southwestern Pacific | 744,100 | 287,300 |
| Madagascar | Indian Ocean | 587,041 | 226,657 |
| Baffin | Canadian Arctic | 507,450 | 195,875 |
| Sumatra | Indian Ocean | 424,760 | 164,000 |
| Honshu | northwestern Pacific | 230,966 | 89,176 |
| Great Britain | northern Atlantic | 218,078 | 84,200 |
| Victoria | Canadian Arctic | 217,206 | 83,896 |
| Ellesmere | Canadian Arctic | 196,160 | 75,767 |

**See also**: *atoll.*

## isobar

Line drawn on maps and weather charts linking all places with the same atmospheric pressure, usually measured in millibars. Isobars are used in weather forecasting.

- Where the isobars are close together, cyclonic weather is indicated, bringing strong winds and a depression.

- Where isobars are far apart, anticyclonic weather is coming, bringing calmer, settled conditions. (*See illustration on opposite page.*)

## isopleth

General term meaning a line on a map which connects points of equal value. Specific types of isopleth include:

- **contour** line, connecting points of equal altitude
- isohyet, connecting points of equal rainfall
- isotherm, connecting points of equal temperature at a given time
- isobath, connecting points of equal distance below a water body
- **isobar**, connecting points of equal atmospheric pressure.

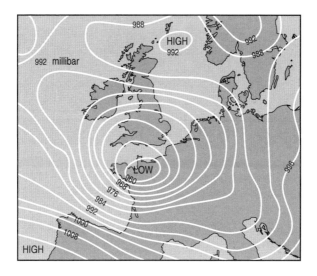

**isobar** *Isobars around a low-pressure area or depression. In the northern hemisphere, winds blow anticlockwise around lows, approximately parallel to the isobars, and clockwise around highs. In the southern hemisphere, the winds blow in the opposite directions.*

## jet stream

The narrow band of very fast wind, with velocities of over 150 kph/95 mph, found at altitudes of 10-16 km/6-10 mi in the upper troposphere or lower stratosphere. Jet streams usually occur about the latitudes of the **westerlies** (35°-60°).

The jet stream may be used by high flying aircraft to speed their journeys. Their discovery of the existence of the jet stream allowed the Japanese to send gas-filled balloons carrying bombs to the northwestern USA during World War II.

## jungle

An area where trees and creepers grow thickly, and where there is abundant wildlife. The term is often used to refer to **rainforests**.

## karst topography

Landscape characterized by remarkable surface and underground forms, created as a result of the action of water on permeable **limestone**. Limestone is soluble in the weak acid of rainwater. Erosion takes place most swiftly along cracks and joints in the limestone and these open up into gullies called grykes. The rounded blocks left upstanding between them are called clints.

The feature takes its name from the Karst region on the Adriatic coast in Slovenia and Croatia, but the name is applied to landscapes throughout the world, the most dramatic of which is found near the city of Guilin in the Guangxi province of China.

**See also:** *limestone.*

## lagoon

Shallow salt water lake, usually with limited access to the sea, or cut off from it by a **coral reef** or barrier **islands**.

## lake

A body of fresh or salt water formed in a hollow in the ground. Lakes are common in **glaciated** regions, along the courses of slow rivers, and in low land near the sea. There are four main types:

- **glacial lakes**, formed by glacial scouring
- **barrier lakes**, formed by **landslides** and glacial **moraines**
- **crater lakes**, found in volcanoes
- **tectonic lakes**, occurring in natural fissures.

Lakes are mainly freshwater, but salt and bitter lakes are found in areas of low annual rainfall and little surface run-off, so that the rate of evaporation exceeds the rate of inflow, allowing mineral salts to accumulate. The Dead Sea has a salinity of about 250 parts per thousand.

## The ten largest lakes in the world

| Lake | Location | Area | |
|---|---|---|---|
| | | sq km | sq mi |
| Caspian Sea | Azerbaijan/Russia/Kazakhstan/Turkmenistan/Iran | 370,990 | 143,239 |
| Superior | USA/Canada | 82,071 | 31,688 |
| Victoria | Tanzania/Kenya/Uganda | 69,463 | 26,820 |
| Aral Sea | Kazakhstan/Uzbekistan | 64,500 | 24,903 |
| Huron | USA/Canada | 59,547 | 22,991 |
| Michigan | USA | 57,735 | 22,291 |
| Tanganyika | Tanzania/Democratic Republic of Congo/Zambia/Burundi | 32,880 | 12,695 |
| Baikal | Russia | 31,499 | 12,162 |
| Great Bear | Canada | 31,316 | 12,091 |
| Malawi (or Nyasa) | Malawi/Tanzania/Mozambique | 28,867 | 11,146 |

In the 20th century, large artificial lakes have been created as a result of hydroelectric and other works. Some lakes have become polluted as a result of human activity.

**See also**: *eutrophication.*

## landform
Part of the land that has a distinct shape, such as a mountain or valley.

## landmark
A feature, such as a hill or a building, that can be seen from a distance. Landmarks are useful in orienteering.

## land reclamation
The conversion of derelict or otherwise unusable areas into productive land. For example, where industrial or agricultural activities such as sand and gravel extraction, or open-cast mining have created large areas of derelict or waste ground, the companies involved are usually required to improve the land so that it can be used.

**See also**: *drainage, polder.*

## landscape
Everything that can be seen in an area of land. An urban landscape consists of buildings and streets, while a rural landscape contains fields, woods, and trees.

## landslide
Sudden downward movement of a mass of soil or rocks from a cliff or steep slope. Landslides happen when a slope becomes unstable, usually because the base has been undercut or because materials within the mass have become wet and slippery. **Earthquakes** may precipitate landslides. (*See illustration on opposite page.*)

## land use
The way in which a given area of land is used. Land is often classified according to its use, for example, for agriculture, industry, residential buildings, and recreation.

## latitude and longitude
Imaginary lines used to locate position on the globe. Lines of latitude are drawn parallel to the **Equator**, with 0° being at the Equator and 90° at the

mudflow landslide

landslip landslide

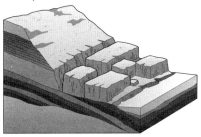

slump landslide

**landslide** *Types of landslide. A mudflow happens when soil or loose material is soaked so that it no longer clings to the slope. It forms a tongue of mud that reaches downhill from a semicircular hollow. A slump occurs when the material stays together as a large mass, or several smaller masses, and these may form a tilted steplike structure as they slide. A landslip is formed when beds of rock dipping towards a cliff slide along a lower bed.*

north and south poles. Lines of longitude are drawn at right angles to these, with 0° being the prime or **Greenwich Meridian**.

---

### THE DEVELOPMENT OF LONGITUDE MEASUREMENT

Until the latter half of the 18th century, sailors navigated by referring to their position east or west of any arbitrary meridian.

Nevil Maskelyne (1732– 1811), English astronomer and fifth Astronomer Royal, referred all of his lunar–stellar distance tables to the Greenwich meridian, so the Greenwich meridian became widely accepted.

Chronometers, time keeping devices with sufficient accuracy for longitude determination, invented by English instrument maker John Harrison (1693–1776) and perfected in 1759, gradually replaced the lunar distance method for navigation.

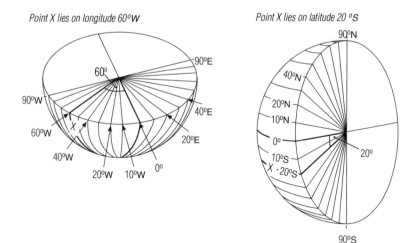

*Point X lies on longitude 60°W*

*Point X lies on latitude 20 °S*

**latitude and longitude** *Locating a point on the globe using latitude and longitude. Longitude is the angle between the terrestrial meridian through a place and the standard meridian 0° passing through Greenwich. Latitude is the angular distance of a place from the Equator.*

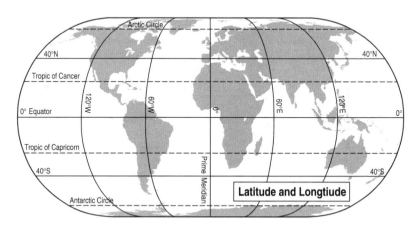

## lava

Molten rock that erupts from a **volcano** and cools to form **igneous rock**. It differs from magma in that it is molten rock on the surface; while **magma** is molten rock below the surface. Lava that is viscous and sticky does not flow far; it forms a steep-sided conical composite volcano, like the island of Montserrat. Less viscous *basalt* lava can flow for long distances and forms a broad flat shield volcano such as those of the Hawaiin islands.

## leaching
Process by which substances are washed through or out of the soil. **Fertilizers** leached from the soil drain into **rivers, lakes**, and ponds and cause **water pollution**. In tropical areas, leaching of the soil after the destruction of **forests** removes scarce nutrients and can lead to a dramatic loss of soil fertility.

## life expectancy
The average number of years that a person may be expected to live from a given age, often birth. Life expectancy depends on nutrition, disease control, environmental contaminants, war, stress, and living standards. It is higher in industrialized countries. In famine-prone Ethiopia, life expectancy from birth is 41 years.

## Countries with the highest life expectancy

### 1995–2000

| *Women* | | *Women* | | *Men* | | *Men* | |
|---|---|---|---|---|---|---|---|
| Japan | 83 | Australia | 81 | Liechtenstein | 78 | Greece | 76 |
| Liechtenstein | 83 | Belgium | 81 | Japan | 77 | Iceland | 76 |
| Monaco | 83 | Canada | 81 | Armenia | 76 | Sweden | 76 |
| Sweden | 82 | France | 81 | Costa Rica | 76 | Australia | 75 |
| Switzerland | 82 | Greece | 81 | Cyprus | 76 | Canada | 75 |

## Countries with the lowest life expectancy

### 1995–2000

| *Women* | | *Women* | | *Men* | | *Men* | |
|---|---|---|---|---|---|---|---|
| Sierra Leone | 43 | Guinea | 47 | Sierra Leone | 40 | Burkina Faso | 45 |
| Uganda | 44 | Guinea-Bissau | 47 | Uganda | 42 | Gambia | 45 |
| Malawi | 45 | Zambia | 47 | Guinea-Bissau | 44 | Mozambique | 45 |
| Afghanistan | 46 | Burkina Faso | 48 | Malawi | 44 | Rwanda | 45 |
| Gambia | 47 | Mozambique | 48 | Afghanistan | 45 | Zambia | 45 |

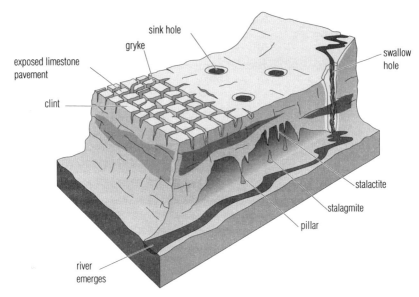

**limestone** *The physical weathering and erosion of a limestone landscape. The freezing and thawing of rain and its mild acidic properties cause cracks and joints to enlarge, forming limestone pavements, potholes, caves, and caverns.*

## limestone

White or grey rock made of the shells of tiny sea creatures and often used in building. **Caves** commonly occur in limestone. Limestone pavements are bare rock surfaces divided into blocks which are separated by joints. Malham Tarn in North Yorkshire is an example of a limestone pavement.

## literacy rate, adult

The ability to read and write, expressed as a percentage of the total adult population of a certain country.

### FACTS ABOUT THE LITERACY RATE

- Nearly one billion people worldwide are illiterate, most of them women.
- Africa has the world's lowest literacy rate, with only 46% of the population able to read and write.
- The level at which the definition of literacy is set will rise as society becomes more complex.
- In 1991, 25 million US adults could not decipher a road sign.

## lithosphere

The topmost layer of the Earth's structure, about 100 km/63 mi thick, which forms the jigsaw of plates that take part in the movements of **plate tectonics**. The lithosphere comprises the **crust** and a portion of the upper mantle. It is regarded as being rigid and moves about on the more elastic and less rigid **asthenosphere**.

## livestock

Animals such as pigs, sheep, and cattle that are reared on farms to provide meat, wool, milk, leather, or dung (for use as fuel). Animal farming involves accommodating and feeding the animals, breeding, gathering produce, slaughtering, and further processing, such as tanning.

**See also**: *agriculture.*

## loess

Yellow soil, originally deposited by a **glacier**, and blown by the wind to the edge of the glaciated region during the **ice ages**. Loess can be very deep, and is very fertile. There are large deposits in central Europe (Hungary), China, and North America.

## longitude

**See** *latitude and longitude.*

## longshore drift

The zigzag movement of sand and pebbles along a **beach**, caused by the action of waves. Longshore drift is responsible for the **erosion** of beaches and the formation of **spits** (ridges of sand or shingle projecting into the water). Attempts are often made to halt longshore drift by erecting barriers, or groynes, at right angles to the shore. (*See illustration on p. 112.*)

**See also**: *backwash, coastal erosion.*

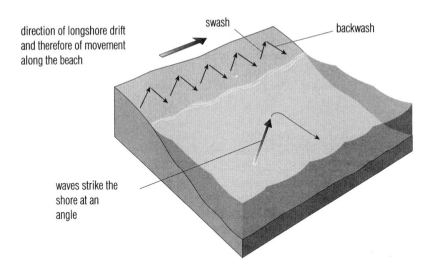

direction of longshore drift
and therefore of movement
along the beach

swash

backwash

waves strike the
shore at an
angle

**longshore drift** *Waves sometimes hit the beach at an angle. The incoming waves (swash) carry sand and shingle up onto the shore and the outgoing wave (backwash) takes some material away with it. Gradually material is carried down the shoreline in the same direction as the longshore current.*

## magma

Molten rock lying under great pressure beneath the **Earth's** surface from which **igneous rocks** are formed. Magma contains silica and basic oxides.
**See also**: *lava*.

## mangrove swamp

Muddy swamp found on tropical coasts and estuaries, characterized by dense thickets of mangrove trees. These low trees are adapted to live in creeks of salt water. Their roots trap silt and mud, creating a firmer, drier environment. Mangrove swamps are common in the Amazon delta and along the coasts of West Africa, northern Australia, and Florida, USA.

## mantle

Part of the **Earth** between the **crust** and the **core**. The boundary between the mantle and the crust above is at an average depth of 32 km/20 mi. The lower boundary with the core is at an average depth of 2,900 km/1,813 mi. The mantle accounts for 82% of Earth's volume and is composed primarily of magnesium, silicon, and oxygen in the form of silicate minerals, such as olivine.

The mantle is subdivided into **upper mantle**, **transition zone**, and **lower mantle.** The upper mantle contains the **asthenosphere**, at 72 km/45 mi to 250 km/155 mi depth, upon which Earth's tectonic plates of **lithosphere** glide. The motions of **plate tectonics** are thought to be influenced by convection currents in the mantle.

## map projection

A way of showing the **Earth's** spherical surface on a flat piece of paper. The most common approach has been to redraw the Earth's surface within a rectangular boundary. The main weakness of this is that countries in high latitudes are shown disproportionately large.There are many types of map projection.

- The most famous cylindrical projection is the Mercator projection, which dates from 1569. Although it gives an exaggerated view of the size of northern continents, it is the best map for navigation as a constant bearing appears as a straight line.

- In 1973 the Peters projection was devised, in which the countries of the world retain their relative areas.

- In other projections, lines of longitude and latitude appear distorted, or the Earth's surface is shown as a series of segments joined along the **Equator**.

- In 1992 the optimal conformal projection was devised, using a computer program designed to take data about the boundary of a given area and calculate the projection that produces the minimum of inaccuracies.

## maps

Diagrammatic representations of areas such as a country or a town. Modern maps are made using a series of overlapping stereoscopic photographs taken by satellites in low orbit, from which a three-dimensional image can be prepared.

---

### FACTS ABOUT MAPS

- The earliest accurate large-scale maps appeared about 1580.
- Conventional aerial photography, laser beams, microwaves, and infrared equipment are also used for land surveying.
- Many different kinds of **map projection** are used in map-making.
- Detailed maps requiring constant updating are kept in digital form on computer so that minor revisions can be made without redrafting.

---

## marble

A rock formed by metamorphism of sedimentary **limestone**. It takes and retains a good polish, and is used in building and sculpture. In its pure form it is white and consists almost entirely of the mineral calcite $CaCO_3$. Mineral impurities give marble various colours and patterns. Carrara, Italy, is known for white marble.

## maritime climate

Mild and damp climate typical of coastal areas because of the nearness of the sea, e.g. most of the UK has a maritime climate.

## market

Any place where buyers and sellers meet to do business with each other. This could range from a street market to a world market where buyers and sellers communicate electronically, or via faxes, telephones, and letters. Markets can be either perfect or imperfect.

- In a perfect or free market, there are many buyers and sellers, so that no single buyer or seller is able to influence the price of the product.

- In an imperfect market a few buyers or sellers, or sometimes just one, dominate the market.

## market gardening

The commercial growing of vegetables, fruit, or flowers. Market gardening is an intensive agriculture system, with crops often being grown inside greenhouses on small farms. Market gardens may be located within easy access of markets, on the fringes of urban areas. Areas where early crops can be grown outside because of a mild climate, are especially suitable.

## marsh

An area of low-lying wetland. Freshwater marshes are common wherever **groundwater**, surface **springs**, streams, or **run-off** cause frequent **flooding** or more or less permanent shallow water. A marsh is alkaline whereas a **bog** is acidic. Marshes develop on inorganic silt or clay soils. Rushes are typical marsh plants. Near the sea, salt marshes may form.

## meander

A loop-shaped curve in a **river** as it follows a winding course across flat country. On the outside of the curve the speed of the **current** is greatest, and so is the **erosion** it causes. On the curve's inside the current is slow and material is deposited, building up a gentle slope. As each meander migrates in the direction of its outer curve, the river gradually changes its course across the flood plain. Meanders are common:

- where the **gradient** is gentle
- where the discharge is fairly steady and not subject to extremes
- where the material carried is fine.

**See also**: *oxbow lake, river.*

## meridian
See *Greenwich Meridian.*

## metamorphic rocks
Rocks of which the structure and composition have been changed by pressure, heat, or chemically active fluids. For example, limestone can be metamorphosed by heat into marble, shale by pressure into slate. There are three main types of metamorphism.

- *Contact metamorphism* occurs when rocks surrounding an **igneous** intrusion are altered as a result of heat.

- *Dislocation metamorphism* takes place as a result of friction along fault or thrust planes.

- *Regional metamorphism* results from the heat and intense pressures associated with the movements and collision of tectonic plates.

  **See also**: *plate tectonics.*

## Main primary material (before metamorphism)

| Typical depth and temperature | Shale with several minerals | Sandstone with only quartz | Limestone with only calcite |
| --- | --- | --- | --- |
| 50,000 ft/570°F | slate | quartzite | marble |
| 65,000 ft/750°F | schist | | |
| 82,000 ft/930°F | gneiss | | |
| 98,500 ft/1,100°F | hornfels | quartzite | marble |

## meteorology
Scientific observation and study of the **atmosphere**, so that **weather** can be accurately forecast. (*See box on opposite page.*)

## microclimate
The climate of a small area, such as a woodland, lake, or even a hedgerow. Significant differences can exist between the climates of two neighbouring areas – for example, a town is usually warmer than the surrounding countryside, and a woodland cooler, darker, and less windy than an area of open land. Microclimates are important in agriculture and horticulture, as different crops require different growing conditions.

**FORECASTING THE WEATHER**

■ Readings are taken of atmospheric pressure, temperature, humidity, **wind, cloud** cover, and **precipitation**.

■ Observations can be collected from land stations, ships, aircraft, and self-recording and automatic transmitting stations. Radar may be used to map clouds and **storms**. Satellites have played an important role in televising pictures of global cloud distribution.

■ Data from meteorological stations and weather satellites is analysed by computers to produce weather maps and forecasts for up to six days ahead.

■ Meteorological observations must be clear, precise, and strictly comparable between stations.

## Mid-Atlantic Ridge

Ocean ridge that runs along the centre of the Atlantic Ocean, parallel to its edges, for some 14,000 km/8,800 mi – almost from the Arctic to the Antarctic. The Mid-Atlantic Ridge is formed by the movement of tectonic plates away from one another at a constructive plate margin. It is central because the ocean crust beneath the Atlantic Ocean has continually grown outwards from the ridge at a steady rate during the past 200 million years. Iceland straddles the ridge and was formed by volcanic outpourings.

**See also:** *plate tectonics.*

## migration

The movement of certain animals, chiefly birds and fish, to distant breeding or feeding grounds. Migration may be seasonal, or part of a single life cycle.

The precise methods by which animals navigate and know where to go are still obscure. Birds have much sharper eyesight and better visual memory of ground clues than humans, but in long-distance flights appear to navigate by the Sun and stars. Leatherback turtles navigate by the contours of underwater mountains and valleys. Most striking, however, is the migration of young birds that have never flown a route before and are unaccompanied by adults. It is thought that they may have a genetically inherited 'sky chart' of their journey.

## mineral

Naturally formed inorganic substance with a particular chemical composition. Rocks are made of minerals. Minerals include quartz, feldspar, calcite, diamond, **coal**, native gold and silver, and gypsum.

---

### MAJOR MINERAL-FORMING PROCESSES

- *Magmatic minerals* crystallize from silica-rich rock melts within the crust or from extruded lavas. Examples include the feldspars, quartz, pyroxenes, amphiboles, micas, and olivines.
- *Sedimentary minerals* form through erosion of rocks exposed at the land surface and transportation by surface waters, ice, or wind to form sediments. These are either pure concentrates or mixtures of sand, clay minerals, and carbonates (chiefly calcite, aragonite, and dolomite).
- *Metamorphic minerals* recrystallize from other minerals because of increasing temperature and pressure with depth in the Earth's crust. Examples include andalusite, cordierite, garnet, wollastonite, chlorite, micas, hornblende, staurolite, kyanite, and diopside.

---

## mining

Extraction of minerals from under the land or sea for industrial or domestic uses. The exhaustion of traditionally accessible resources such as coal has led to development of new mining techniques; for example, extraction of oil from offshore deposits and from land shale reserves. Technology is also being developed to extract minerals from entirely new sources such as mud deposits and mineral nodules from the sea bed.

## mist

Low **cloud** caused by the condensation of water vapour in the lower part of the **atmosphere**. Mist is less thick than **fog**, and reduces visibility to 1–2 km or about one mile.

## monsoon

A **wind** of southern **Asia** that blows towards the sea in winter and towards the land in summer and brings seasonally heavy rainfall. The monsoon may cause destructive **flooding** all over India and Southeast Asia from April to September, leaving thousands of people homeless each year.

## moorland

A stretch of land, usually in the mountains, where heather, coarse grass, and bracken grow. A moor may be cold and windswept, and may be poorly drained with boggy hollows. More than 50% of Scotland is regarded as moorland.

## moraine

Rocky debris carried along and deposited by a **glacier**.

- Lateral moraine is material eroded from the side of a glaciated valley and carried along the glacier's edge.
- Ground moraine is that worn from the valley floor and carried along the base of the glacier.
- Terminal moraine is dropped at the snout of a melting glacier.
- Medial moraine forms when lateral moraine from two glaciers meets.

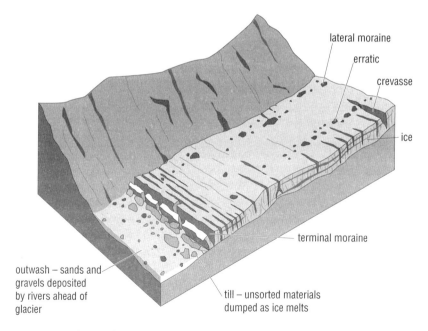

**moraine**  *A glacier picks up large boulders and rock debris from the valley and deposits them at the snout of the glacier when the ice melts (terminal moraine) or along the side of the glacier (lateral moraine). Some material is carried great distances by the ice to form erratics.*

- Englacial moraine is debris that has fallen down crevasses and become embedded in the ice.

## mountain

A large mass of upland, higher and steeper than a hill. Mountains are at least 330 m/1000 ft above the surrounding **topography**. Mountains are built by the actions of **volcanoes**, and from folding, faulting, thrusting, and uplift when two continental plates collide at a convergent margin. The existing rock is often subjected to high temperatures and pressures which form metamorphic rock, and the intrusion of igneous rock such as granite can also accompany mountain formation.

**See also**: *plate tectonics*.

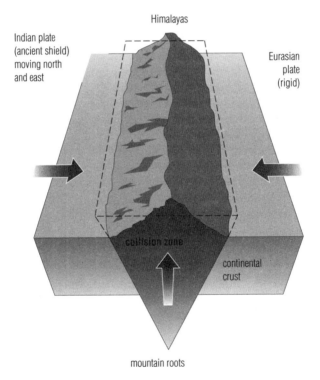

**mountain** *Mountains are created when two tectonic plates collide and no subduction takes place. The crust at the collision zone is squeezed together and thrust upwards.*

## Highest mountains in the world

| Mountain | Location | Height | |
|----------|----------|--------|---|
| | | **m** | **ft** |
| Everest | China/Nepal | 8,848 | 29,028 |
| K2 | Kashmir/ Jammu | 8,611 | 28,251 |
| Kangchenjunga | India/Nepal | 8,598 | 28,202 |
| Lhoste | China/Nepal | 8,511 | 27,923 |
| Yaling Kang | India/Nepal | 8,502 | 27,,893 |
| McKinley | Alaska, USA | 6,194 | 20,321 |
| Logan, Yukon | Canada | 6,050 | 19,849 |
| Kilimanjaro | Tanzania | 5,895 | 19,337 |
| Elbrus, West Peak | Russia | 5,642 | 18,510 |
| Citlaltépetl | Mexico | 5,610 | 18,405 |

## multinational corporation

Company or enterprise that operates in several countries, usually defined as one with 25% or more of its output capacity located outside its country of origin.

---

### FACTS ABOUT MULTINATIONAL CORPORATIONS

■ The world's four largest multinationals in 1994 were General Motors, Ford, Exxon, and Shell. Their total sales exceeded the **gross national product** of all of Africa.

■ The top 100 multinationals in 1994 controlled $3.4 trillion in financial assets.

■ In 1993, multinationals accounted for one-third of the world's industrial output, with sales of $4,800 billion.

■ Multinationals are seen in some quarters as posing a threat to individual national sovereignty and as exerting undue influence to secure favourable operating conditions. Unsuccessful efforts were made in 1992 to negotiate a voluntary code of conduct for multinationals, but governments and corporations alike were hostile to the idea.

---

## national park

Land set aside and conserved for public enjoyment. National parks include not only the most scenic places, but also places distinguished by their historic, prehistoric, or scientific interest, or for their superior recreational assets. They range from areas the size of small countries to pockets of just a few hectares. Yellowstone National Park, USA, was the first national park, established in 1872. National parks in the UK include the Peak District, the Lake District, and Snowdonia.

## natural gas

Mixture of flammable gases found in the **Earth's** crust, often in association with petroleum. With coal and oil, natural gas is one of the world's three main **fossil fuels**.

---

### FACTS ABOUT NATURAL GAS

- Natural gas is a mixture of hydrocarbons, chiefly methane (80%), with ethane, butane, and propane.
- It is usually transported from its source by pipeline.
- Natural gas may be liquefied for transport and storage and is often used in remote areas where other fuels are scarce and expensive.
- In the UK natural gas from the North Sea has superseded coal gas, both as a domestic fuel and as an energy source for power stations.

---

## natural hazard

A naturally occurring phenomenon capable of causing destruction, injury, disease, or death. Examples include **earthquakes, floods, hurricanes**, and **famine**. Natural hazards occur globally and can play an important role in shaping the **landscape**. The events only become hazards where people are affected. Because of this, natural hazards are usually measured in terms of the damage they cause to persons or property. Human activities can trigger natural hazards, for example skiers crossing the top of a snowpack may cause an **avalanche**.

## nature reserve
Area set aside to protect a habitat and the wildlife that lives within it. A nature reserve often provides a sanctuary for rare species, and public admission is restricted. The world's largest is Etosha Reserve, Namibia, with an area of 99,520 sq km/38,415 sq mi.

## newly-industrializing countries
Countries formerly classified as less developed, but which are becoming rapidly industrialized. The first wave of countries to be identified as newly-industrializing included Hong Kong, South Korea, Singapore, and Taiwan. These countries underwent rapid industrial growth in the 1970s and 1980s, attracting significant financial investment, and are now associated with high-technology industries. More recently, Thailand, China, and Malaysia have been classified as newly-industrializing countries.

## nomad
Person who, instead of settling permanently in one spot, moves freely from place to place according to the availability of grazing or food. Nomads fall into two main groups:
- herders
- **hunter-gatherers**.

Both groups are threatened by enclosure of land and by the destruction of habitats, as well as by the social and economic pressures of a capitalist economy.

## non-governmental organization (NGO)
Independent, service-providing organization engaged in a range of activities, including the provision of aid to less developed countries. Examples include Oxfam, the Red Cross, and Greenpeace.

## nonrenewable resources
Natural resources, such as **coal** or **oil**, that cannot be replaced once consumed because they takes thousands or millions of years to form naturally. The main **energy sources** used by humans are nonrenewable. Renewable energy resources, such as solar, tidal, and geothermal power, have so far been less exploited.

## North America

North America is third largest of all the continents, connected by the isthmus of Panama to the continent of South America, and comprises Greenland, Canada, the United States and Mexico, as well as Central America. Its total population is 450 million. With an overall length of over 8,000 km/4,970 mi, North America has a wide range of **climates**, resulting in zones of different soils and **vegetation**. The northernmost areas are cold and sparsely populated. Temperatures rise above freezing only between June and September. Caribou and musk oxen live here, and the landscape comprises moorland and coniferous forest. The central part of North America has an agricultural heartland known as the Great Plains, characterized by treeless expanses crossed by broad, shallow river valleys. The climate is semi-arid.

A warm temperate zone covers the marshy southern lowlands of the Mississippi, one of the longest **rivers** in the world, and the southeastern USA and is dominated by the Gulf tropical air mass. Winters are mild and the frost-free season lasts over 200 days. The southwestern USA experiences a Mediterranean-type climate, with dry summers and mild winters. The eastern side of Mexico, and the lands of Central America have a hot and wet tropical climate. There are also climatic pockets, such as the subtropical southern tip of Florida and the deserts of the Southwest.

Animals found in North America range from caribou and wolves in the cold northern wastelands, and mountain lions, bears, and lynxes in the mountains, to coyotes, prairie dogs, bison, and antelope in the prairies. The Florida Everglades are home to a unique variety of reptiles, such as aligators, crocodiles, and snakes, and wading birds, including flamingoes and herons.

The Rocky Mountains run parallel to the west coast of North America, and include Mount McKinley at 6,194 m/20,316 ft. The Grand Canyon, deepest in the world, is also in the west of the continent. The Great Lakes between the USA and Canada are another outstanding geographical feature, which are large and deep enough to allow the passage of shipping.

---

**PRODUCTS OF NORTH AMERICA**

| Country | Products |
|---------|----------|
| Canada | nickel, zinc, uranium, potash, linseed, asbestos, silver, titanium |
| USA | salt, oil, cotton, beef, veal |
| Mexico | silver, oil |

The USA has abundant resources and an expanding home market. Its fast-growing industrial and technological strength has made it less dependent on exports.

North America is made up of three major structural areas:

- the North American craton
- the Appalachian fold belt, which abuts the southeast margin of the craton
- the Cordilleran fold belt, which lies along the southwest margin of the craton.

The North American craton is an ancient shield area which occupies the major part of the north of the continent, tapering towards the south in an inverted triangle.

In the east are the Appalachian Mountains, flanked by the narrow coastal plain which widens further south. Erosion here has created a line of planed crests, or terraces, at altitudes between 300-1,200 m/985-3,935 ft. This has also formed a ridge-and-valley topography which was an early barrier to continental penetration. Low plains on the Atlantic coast are indented by the Gulf of St Lawrence, Bay of Fundy, Delaware Bay, and Chesapeake Bay.

The western cordillera, a mountain belt running parallel to the coast from Alaska to Panama, is perhaps the most dominating structure of North America. It is called the Rocky Mountains in the USA and Canada and its continuation into Mexico is called the Sierra Madre. Rivers rising on the east slopes have a long way to go to the sea, and the drainage basins of these large rivers (such as the Mackenzie) are enormous. While the rivers

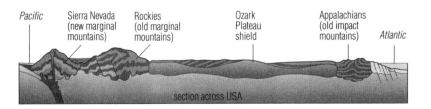

**North America** *The North American continent is growing in the west as a result of collision with the Pacific plate. On the east of the wide area of the Ozark Plateau shield lie the Appalachian Mountains, showing where the continent once collided with another continent. The eastern coastal rifting formed when the two continents broke apart to form the Atlantic Ocean. On the western edge, new mountains have formed.*

flowing east are the largest, the rivers flowing west (the Colorado, Columbia, and the Frazer), cutting through the western cordillera, are the most spectacular.

To the east of the cordillera lie the Great Plains, the agricultural heartland of North America, which descend in a series of steps to the depressions occupied by the Great Lakes in the east and the Gulf of Mexico coastal lowlands in the southeast.

## nuclear energy

Energy derived from splitting or combining the nuclei of atoms. There are two main types.

- **Nuclear fission**, produces huge amounts of energy by splitting the nuclei of atoms of a material such as uranium or plutonium. The process is controlled inside the reactor of a nuclear power plant by absorbing excess neutrons in control rods and slowing down their speed.

- **Nuclear fusion** releases energy when hydrogen nuclei fuse to helium nuclei, and is the principle behind the hydrogen bomb. Attempts to harness fusion for commercial power production have so far been unsuccessful.

    **See also:** *energy resources.*

## nuclear power

Nuclear power is electricity generated in power stations as a result of the nuclear fission process. The major fuel is uranium which is converted to uranium dioxide before undergoing nuclear fission. Nuclear power stations are expensive to build and decommission but are relatively cheap to run and use small amounts of uranium, which is abundant. The possible safety risks and the need for large quantities of cooling water mean that nuclear power plants are often located in relatively remote, coastal areas.

In Britain approximately 20% of electricity is generated by nuclear reactors. In France the figure is more than 70%.

Many governments curtailed or cancelled their nuclear power programmes in the 1980s due to increasing costs, problems with disposing of radioactive waste, and environmental concerns triggered by incidents such as the Chernobyl disaster in 1986, when a nuclear reactor exploded and caught fire, producing a radioactive cloud that spread from the site across parts of Europe and Asia.

## nutrient cycle

The transfer of nutrients from one part of an **ecosystem** to another. Trees, for example, take up nutrients such as calcium and potassium from the soil through their root systems and store them in leaves. When the leaves fall they are decomposed by bacteria and the nutrients are released back into the soil where they become available for root uptake again.

## oasis

An area in a desert made fertile by the presence of water near the surface. The occurrence of oases affects the distribution of plants, animals, and people in the desert regions of the world.

## ocean

The great mass of salt water that surrounds the continents. There are four areas of ocean – the **Atlantic**, **Indian**, **Pacific**, and Arctic. Together they cover approximately 70% of the **Earth's** surface. Water levels in the world's oceans have increased by 10–15 cm/4–6 in over the past 100 years.

> ❢ How inappropriate to call this planet Earth when quite clearly it is an Ocean. ❡
>
> **Arthur C Clarke**, *Nature*, 1990

---

**FACTS ABOUT OCEANS**

*Depth* The average depth is 3,660 m/12,000 ft, but shallow ledges of 180 m/600 ft depth run out from the continents. Only the **deep-sea trenches** go deeper.

*Features* Deep trenches (off eastern and southeast Asia, and western South America), volcanic belts (in the western Pacific and eastern Indian Ocean), and ocean ridges (in the mid-Atlantic, eastern Pacific, and Indian Ocean).

*Temperature* Temperature varies on the surface with latitude (–2°C to +29°C).

*Water contents* Salinity averages about 3%; minerals commercially extracted include bromine, magnesium, potassium, and salt.

*Pollution* Ocean pollutants include airborne emissions from land; oil from both shipping and land-based sources; toxins from industrial, agricultural, and domestic uses; **sewage**; sediments from mining, **forestry**, and farming; plastic litter; and radioactive isotopes.

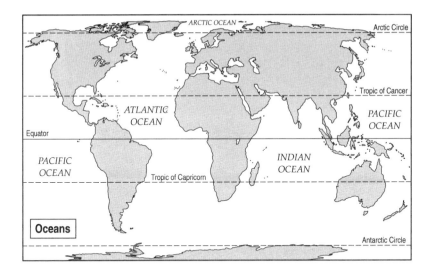

**Oceans**

---

**FEATURES OF THE OCEAN FLOOR**

- **ocean ridge**
- **abyssal plain**
- **seamount**
- **guyot**
- **deep-sea trench**
- continental margin including the **continental slope**, and **continental shelf**.

---

**See also**: *arctic, current, Gulf Stream.*

## ocean ridge

Mountain range on the seabed indicating the presence of a constructive plate margin, where tectonic plates are moving apart and magma rises to the surface. Ocean ridges, such as the **Mid-Atlantic Ridge**, consist of many segments offset along transform **faults**, and can rise thousands of metres above the surrounding seabed.

Ocean ridges usually have a **rift valley** along their crests, indicating where the flanks are being pulled apart by the growth of the plates. The crests are generally free of sediment; increasing depths of sediment are found with increasing distance down the flanks.

**See also:** *plate tectonics.*

## ocean trench
See *deep-sea trench.*

## Oceania
General or collective name for the groups of islands in the southern and central Pacific Ocean, comprising all those intervening between the southeastern shores of Asia and the western shores of America. The 10,000 or more Pacific Islands offer a great diversity of environments, from almost barren, waterless coral **atolls** to vast, continental islands.

Oceania can be broadly divided into groups of volcanic and coral islands on the basis of the ethnic origins of their inhabitants:

- Micronesia, including Guam, Kiribati, Mariana, Marshall, and Caroline Islands
- Melanesia, which includes Papua New Guinea, Vanuatu, New Caledonia, Fiji Islands, and the Solomon Islands
- Polynesia, including Tonga, Samoa, Line Islands, Tuvalu, French Polynesia, and Pitcairn Island.

## oil
A thick greenish-brown flammable liquid found underground in permeable rocks and known as crude oil or petroleum. It consists of naturally occur-

---

**FACTS ABOUT OIL**

- Petroleum is often found trapped below layers of rock as large lakes floating on water under a layer of natural gas.
- It may flow naturally from wells under gas pressure from above, or water pressure from below, causing it to rise up the borehole, but many wells require pumping to bring it to the surface.
- Products such as fuel oil, petrol, kerosene, diesel, lubricating oil, paraffin wax, and petroleum jelly are made by distillation of petroleum.
- Petroleum products and chemicals are used in the manufacture of detergents, artificial fibres, plastics, insecticides, **fertilizers**, pharmaceuticals, toiletries, and synthetic rubber.
- The burning of oil-based fuels is a major cause of **air pollution**.

ring hydrocarbons and is derived from organic material laid down millions of years ago.

## ore
Body of rock, a vein within a rock, or a deposit of sediment, containing valuable metals.

- Some ore deposits are formed when fluids such as saline water pass through fissures in the rock at a high temperature. Other ores are concentrated by igneous processes, which cause the ore metals to become segregated from a **magma**.
- Ores often contain unwanted impurities that must be removed when the metal is extracted.
- Commercially valuable ores include bauxite, from which aluminium is made, haematite, which contains iron, and zinc.

## organic farming
Farming without the use of artificial **fertilizers**, **pesticides**, or other agro-chemicals.

- In place of artificial fertilizers, compost, manure, or seaweed are used.
- Growing a crop of a nitrogen-fixing plant (legume), then ploughing it back into the soil, also fertilizes the ground.
- Weeds can be controlled by hoeing, mulching (covering with manure, straw, or black plastic), or burning off.
- Organic farming methods produce food with minimal pesticide residues and greatly reduce pollution of the environment. They are more labour intensive and therefore more expensive, but use less **fossil fuel**.
  **See also**: *agriculture, crops.*

## orogeny or orogenesis
The formation of mountains. It is brought about by the movements of the rigid plates making up the Earth's **crust** and upper-most **mantle**, in the process of **plate tectonics**. Where two plates collide at a destructive margin rocks become folded and lifted to form chains of mountains, such as the Himalayas.

Processes associated with orogeny are faulting and thrusting, folding, metamorphism, and plutonism. However, many topographical features of mountains – cirques, u-shaped valleys – are the result of *non-orogenic* processes, such as **weathering**, **erosion**, and **glaciation**. Uplift due to the buoyancy of the Earth's crust can also influence mountain physiography.

    **See also:** *fault, fold mountain, igneous rock.*

## overpopulation

A state of having too many people living in an area than can be supported by the resources available such as food, land, and water. Although there is often a link between overpopulation and population density, high densities will not always result in overpopulation.

---

**OVERPOPULATION AND POPULATION DENSITY**

- In many countries, resources are plentiful and the **infrastructure** and technology are well developed. This means that a large number of people can be supported by a small area of land.
- In some countries, such as Bangladesh, Ethiopia, and Brazil, insufficient food, minerals, and energy, and inequitable income distribution result in poverty and often migration in search of better living conditions. Here even low population densities may amount to overpopulation.
- Overpopulation may also result from a decrease in resources or an increase in population or a combination of both.

---

    **See also:** *population.*

## oxbow lake

Curved lake found on the **flood plain** of a **river**. Oxbows are caused by the loops of **meanders** being cut off at times of **flood** and the river subsequently adopting a shorter course. (*See illustration on opposite page.*)

## ozone layer

Thin layer of the gas ozone in the upper **atmosphere** that shields the **Earth** from harmful ultraviolet rays. A continent-sized hole has formed over Antarctica as a result of damage to the ozone layer. This has been caused in part by **CFCs**, but many other reactions destroy ozone.

    **See also:** *global warming, greenhouse effect.*

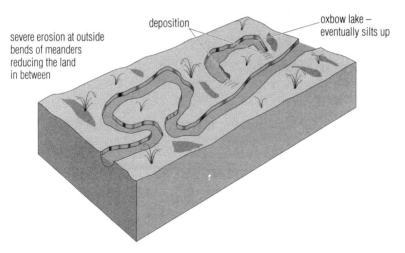

severe erosion at outside bends of meanders reducing the land in between

deposition

oxbow lake – eventually silts up

**oxbow lake** *The formation of an oxbow lake. As a river meanders across a flood plain, the outer bends are gradually eroded and the water channel deepens; as the loops widen, the neck of the loop narrows and finally gives way, allowing the water to flow in a more direct route, isolating the old water channel and forming an oxbow lake.*

## THE DESTRUCTION OF THE OZONE LAYER

- The ozone layer is depleting at a rate of about 5% every 10 years over northern Europe.
- Ozone depletion over the **polar** regions is the most dramatic manifestation of a general global effect. Ozone levels over the **Arctic** in spring 1997 had fallen over 10 % since 1987.
- It is expected that an Arctic hole as large as that over Antarctica could remain a threat to the northern hemisphere for several decades.
- The size of the hole in the ozone layer was three times the size of the USA, in October 1998. This is bigger than it has ever been before and may be due to the adverse effects of **El Niño** on the climate.

## Pacific Ocean

World's largest and deepest ocean, extending from Antarctica to the Bering Strait. The Pacific is the deepest ocean; with an average depth 4,188 m/ 13,749 ft. It has several **deep-sea trenches**, e.g. the Mariana Trench (11,034 m/ 36,200 ft).

- *Currents* Winds in the northern Pacific produce clockwise currents.
- *Islands* There are over 2,500 islands in the central and western regions, of volcanic or coral origin, many being **atolls**. The Pacific is ringed by an area of volcanic activity, with accompanying **earthquakes**.

## pastoral agriculture

A type of farming where the raising of livestock predominates.
  **See also**: *farming types.*

## peat

Dark brown, fibrous organic substance found in **bogs** and formed from partially decomposed plants such as sphagnum moss. Peat has been dried and used as fuel from ancient times, and can also be used as a soil additive. Northern Asia, Canada, Finland, Ireland, and other places have large deposits.

---

### THE DESTRUCTION OF PEAT BOGS

- Peat bogs began to be formed when **glaciers** retreated, about 9,000 years ago.
- They grow at the rate of only one millimetre a year, and large-scale digging can result in destruction both of the bog and of specialized plants growing there.
- The destruction of peat bogs is responsible for diminishing fish stocks in coastal waters. The run-off from the peatlands carries high concentrations of iron, which affects the growth of the plankton on which the fish feed.

## pediment
Broad, gently sloping surface formed at the base of a **mountain** as it erodes and retreats. Pediments consist of bedrock and are often covered with a thin layer of **sediment**, called alluvium, which has been eroded off the mountain.

## peninsula
Land surrounded on three sides by water but still attached to a larger landmass. Florida, USA, is an example.

## periglacial
Having similar climatic and environmental characteristics to a glacial area, such as mountain regions, or bordering a glacial area but not actually covered by ice. Examples are parts of Siberia, Greenland, and North America. The rock and soil in these areas are frozen to a depth of several metres (**permafrost**) with only the top few centimetres thawing during the brief summer. The vegetation is characteristic of **tundra**.

   **See also**: *glacier and glaciation.*

## permafrost
Condition in which a deep layer of soil does not thaw out during the summer. Permafrost occurs under **periglacial** conditions. Around 26% of the world's land surface is permafrost. It produces a poorly drained form of grassland typical of northern Canada, Siberia, and Alaska known as tundra.

## permeable and impermeable rock
Permeable rocks, such as **limestone** and chalk, allow water to soak in, while impermeable rocks do not.

* In permeable rocks, such as **sandstone**, water can pass through either via a network of spaces between particles, or along bedding planes, cracks, and fissures. Permeable rocks can become saturated.

* Impermeable rocks do not have bedding planes, joints, fissures, or pores, so the passage of water through the rock is prevented; for example, mudstones and shales.

   **See also**: *pervious and impervious rocks.*

## pervious and impervious rock

- Pervious rocks allow the passage of water through bedding planes, cracks, and fissures, but are non-porous, as in some limestones.
- Impervious rocks do not allow the passage of water.

**See also**: *permeable and impermeable rocks.*

## pesticides

Any chemicals used in farming, gardening, or indoors to combat pests. Pesticides cause a number of pollution problems through spray drift onto surrounding areas, direct contamination of users or the public, and as residues on food. The World Health Organization (WHO) estimated in 1999 that 20,000 people worldwide die annually from pesticide poisoning incidents.

There are three main types of pesticide:

- **insecticides,** to kill insects
- **fungicides**, to kill fungal diseases
- **herbicides**, to kill plants, mainly those considered weeds.

## petroleum

See *oil.*

## pH scale

Scale ranging from 0 to 14, for measuring acidity or alkalinity. A pH of 7.0 indicates neutrality, below 7 is acid, while above 7 is alkaline.

- Strong acids, such as those used in car batteries, have a pH of about 2.
- Acidic fruits such as citrus fruits are about pH 4.
- Strong alkalis such as sodium hydroxide are pH 13.

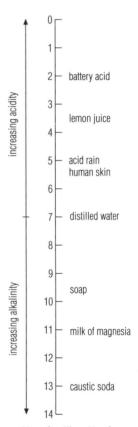

**pH scale** *The pHs of some common substances. The lower the pH is, the more acidic the substance; the higher the pH, the more alkaline the substance.*

- Weak alkalis such as soap are pH 9 to 10.
- Fertile soils have a pH of 6.5 to 7.0.

The pH of a solution can be measured by using a solution or paper strip which is a broad-range indicator. The colour produced by the indicator is compared with a colour code related to the pH value. An alternative method is to use a pH meter fitted with a glass electrode.

**See also:** *acid rain.*

### photosynthesis

Process by which green plants use light energy from the Sun to create carbohydrates. The carbohydrates occur in the form of simple sugar, or glucose, which provides the basic food for both plants and animals. For photosynthesis to occur, the plant must possess chlorophyll and must have a supply of carbon dioxide and water. Photosynthesis takes place inside chloroplasts which are found mainly in the leaf cells of plants.

The by-product of photosynthesis, oxygen, is of great importance to all living organisms, and virtually all atmospheric oxygen originates from photosynthesis.

### plantation

Large farm or estate where one crop is commercially produced. Examples of crops produced on plantations are rubber, in Malaysia, palm oil, in Nigeria, or tea, in Sri Lanka. Plantations are usually owned by large companies, often **multinational corporations**, and run by an estate manager. Many plantations were established in countries under colonial rule, using slave labour.

**See also**: *colonialism.*

### plateau

High area of flat land, or a mountainous region in which the peaks are at the same height. Examples of plateaus are the Tibetan Plateau and the Massif Central in France. There are three types of plateau.

- An intermontane plateau is surrounded by mountains.
- A piedmont plateau lies between the mountains and low-lying land.
- A continental plateau rises abruptly from low-lying lands or the sea.

## plate tectonics

Theory formulated in the 1960s to explain **continental drift** and seafloor spreading, and the formation of the major physical features of the **Earth's** surface.

There are three types of plate margins:

- *Constructive margins* Where two plates are moving apart from each other, molten rock from the mantle wells up in the space between the plates and hardens to form new crust, usually in the form of an **ocean ridge** (such as the **Mid-Atlantic Ridge**). The newly formed crust accumulates on either side of the ocean ridge, causing the sea floor to spread. The process is sometimes referred to as seafloor spreading. The floor of the Atlantic Ocean is growing by 5 cm/2 in each year because of the welling-up of new material at the Mid-Atlantic Ridge.

- *Destructive margins* Where two plates are moving towards each other, the denser of the two plates may be forced under the other into a region called the subduction zone, marked by a **deep-sea trench**. The descending plate melts to form a body of magma, which may then rise to the surface through cracks and faults to form volcanoes. If the two plates consist of more buoyant continental crust, subduction does not occur. Instead, the crust crumples gradually to form ranges of young mountains, such as the Himalayas.

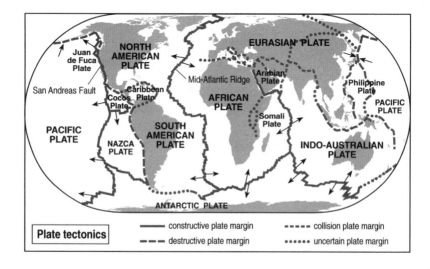

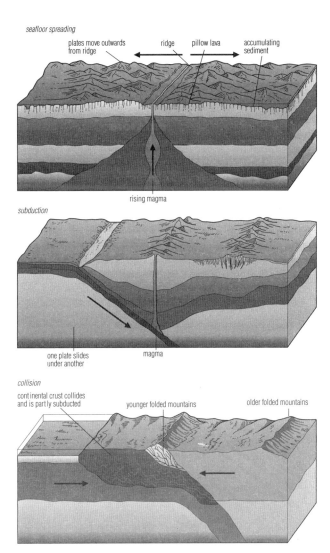

*seafloor spreading*

plates move outwards from ridge — ridge — pillow lava — accumulating sediment

rising magma

*subduction*

one plate slides under another — magma

*collision*

continental crust collides and is partly subducted — younger folded mountains — older folded mountains

**plate tectonics** *Constructive and destructive action in plate tectonics. Top: Seafloor spreading. The upwelling of magma forces the plates to rift apart, producing new crust at the joint. Rapid extrusion of magma produces a domed ridge; more gentle rifting produces a central valley. Middle: The drawing downwards of an oceanic plate beneath a continental plate produces a range of volcanic mountains parallel to the plate edge. Bottom: Collision of two continental plates produces immense fold mountains such as the Himalayas. Younger mountains are found near the coast with older ranges inland.*

• *Conservative margins* Sometimes two plates will slide past each other –
an example is the San Andreas Fault in California, where the movement
of the plates sometimes takes the form of sudden jerks, causing the earthquakes common in the San Francisco–Los Angeles area.

---

**FACTS ABOUT PLATE TECTONICS**

■ The outermost layer of the Earth is regarded as a jigsaw puzzle of six or
seven large plates and a number of smaller ones. These plates move,
probably under the combined influence of convection currents in the
**mantle** beneath, and the pull on the plate caused by those areas being
actively drawn underneath adjacent plates.

■ The rate of plate movement is at most 15 cm/6 in per year.

■ At their margins, where plates collide or move apart, major landforms
such as **mountains, volcanoes, deep-sea trenches**, and **ocean ridges**
are created.

■ The margins of the plates are defined by major earthquake zones and
belts of volcanic and tectonic activity, which have been well known for
many years. Almost all earthquake, volcanic, and tectonic activity is
confined to the margins of plates, and shows that the plates are in
constant motion.

---

## polder
Area of flat, reclaimed land that used to be covered by a **river, lake**, or the
**sea**. Polders have been artificially drained and protected from flooding by
building dykes. They are common in the Netherlands, where the total land
area has been increased by nearly one-fifth since AD 1200. Reclamation
schemes such as the Zuider Zee project have provided some of the best
agricultural land in the country.

## polar
The areas around the North and South Poles.
    **See also**: *pole.*

## pole
The geographic north and south points at each end of the **Earth's** axis. The
North Pole lies beneath the Arctic Ocean, the South Pole is beneath

**Antarctica**. The geographic poles differ from the magnetic poles, which are the points towards which a freely suspended magnetic needle will point and which vary in their location through time.

## pollution

Contamination of the environment by elements such as noise, smoke, car emissions, chemical and radioactive effluents, **pesticides**, radiation, sewage, and household waste. These may result from human activity, such as industry, or natural events, such as volcanic eruptions. Pollution contributes to the **greenhouse effect**.

- Pollution control involves higher production costs for the industries concerned.

- Failure to implement adequate controls may result in irreversible environmental damage and an increase in the incidence of diseases such as cancer.

- Radioactive pollution results from inadequate nuclear safety.

- The existence of 1,300 toxic waste tips in the UK in 1990 posed a considerable threat for increased water pollution.

   **See also**: *acid rain, air pollution.*

## population

The members of a given species, living in a certain area and able to interbreed. The world population refers to the number of people alive in the world at a given time. (*See maps on p. 142.*)

   **See also**: *birth rate, death rate, demographic transition, life expectancy.*

### Growth in world population

| Date | Estimated world population | Date | Estimated world population |
|------|---------------------------|------|---------------------------|
| 1900 | 1,620,000,000 | 1980 | 4,450,000,000 |
| 1950 | 2,500,000,000 | 1990 | 5,245,000,000 |
| 1960 | 3,050,000,000 | 2000 | 6,100,000,000 |
| 1970 | 3,700,000,000 | | |

## port

Place where goods are loaded onto or unloaded from ships in order to be transported by land. Most ports are coastal, though inland ports on rivers

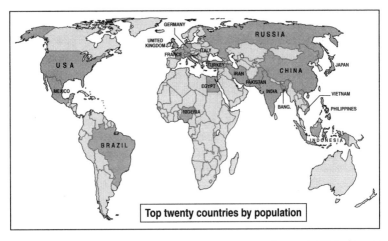

**population** *A comparison of the top twenty countries by population and by area shows that some of the countries with the largest populations have the smallest areas and vice versa.*

also exist. Ports often have specialized equipment, such as container or roll-on/roll-off facilities in order to handle large quantities of cargo. Historically, ports have been important starting points from which the transport networks of many colonial and trading countries developed.

## power station

Building where electrical energy is generated from a fuel or from another form of energy. The energy supply is used to turn turbines either directly by means of water or wind pressure, or indirectly by pressure from steam generated by burning fossil fuels or from the heat released by the fission of uranium nuclei. The turbines spin alternators, which generate electricity at very high voltage.

- Fuels used include **fossil fuels** such as **coal**, gas, and oil, and the nuclear fuel uranium.
- Renewable sources of energy include water, used to produce **hydroelectric power**, and wind.
- According to a report by the Office of National Statistics 1996, power stations produce a quarter of all greenhouse emissions, and nearly half of the **acid rain** emissions, in the UK.

  **See also**: *energy resources, greenhouse effect.*

## prairie

Level areas of grassland in the USA. The central North American prairie extends over most of the region between the Rocky Mountains, to the west, and the Great Lakes and Ohio River, to the east. Once grass-covered, this prairie has now been altered by farming into the 'Corn Belt', much of the 'Wheat Belt', and other ploughed lands. Its humus-rich black **loess** soils, adequate rainfall, and warm summers make it heavily productive. The prairies were formerly the primary habitat of the American bison; other prominent species include prairie dogs, deer and antelope, grasshoppers, and a variety of prairie birds.

## precipitation

Water that falls to the **Earth** from the **atmosphere** as **rain**, snow, sleet, hail, **dew**, and frost. It is part of the **hydrological cycle**.

- The amount of precipitation in any one area depends on **climate**, **weather**, and phenomena like **trade winds** and ocean **currents**.
- **El Niño** causes dramatic shifts in the amount of precipitation in South and Central America and throughout the Pacific region.
- Precipitation can also be influenced by people. In urban areas dust, smoke, and other pollution cause water in the air to condense more readily.

## quarry

Place usually in the open air from which stone, gravel, and **minerals** are excavated. The suitability of stone for quarrying depends on its quality, inclination, and depth below the surface, and possibility of cheap and easy transport to a large market. The main deposits worked by quarrying are **sandstones**, **limestones**, marble, ironstones, slates, and **granite**.

## quartz

One of the most commonest minerals in nature. Quartz is the crystalline form of silica, silicon dioxide, and occurs in many different kinds of rock, including sandstone and granite. Quartz is very hard and is resistant to chemical or mechanical breakdown.

Crystals of pure quartz are coarse, colourless, transparent, show no cleavage, and fracture unevenly; this form is called rock crystal. Impure coloured varieties, often used as gemstones, include agate and amethyst.

# R

## race

A group of people of common descent, having distinctive physical traits in common. During the last 60,000 years, migrations and interbreeding have caused a range of variations to exist today, rather than distinct races, which can exist only under conditions of isolation. Race is a cultural, political, and economic concept, not a biological one. Most anthropologists completely reject the concept of race, and social scientists tend to prefer the term **ethnic group**.

## railway

Method of transport in which trains convey passengers and goods along a twin rail track.

---

### THE RISE AND DECLINE OF RAILWAYS

- The first public steam railway in England was opened in 1825. This heralded extensive railway building in Britain, continental Europe, and North America, providing a fast and economical means of transport and communication.
- After World War II, steam engines were replaced by electric and diesel engines. At the same time, the growth of road building, air services, and car ownership brought to an end the supremacy of the railways.

---

## rain

Form of **precipitation** in which separate drops of water fall to the **Earth's** surface from **clouds**. The drops are formed by the accumulation of fine droplets that condense from water vapour in the air. The **condensation** is usually brought about by rising and subsequent cooling of air. There are three main types of rainfall.

- *Frontal rainfall* takes place at the **front** between a mass of warm air from the tropics and a mass of cold air from the poles. The water vapour in the warm air is chilled and condenses to form clouds and rain.

- *Orographic rainfall* occurs when an airstream is forced to rise over a mountain range. The air becomes cooled and rain falls.

- *Convectional rainfall*, associated with hot climates and usually accompanied by a thunderstorm, is brought about by rising and abrupt cooling of air that has been warmed by the extreme heat of the ground surface. The water vapour carried by the air condenses and so rain falls heavily.

## rainforest

Dense forest usually found on or near the **Equator** where the climate is hot and wet. Moist air brought by the converging **trade winds** rises because of the heat, producing heavy rainfall. Tropical rainforests are characterized by a great diversity of species, usually of tall broad-leafed evergreen trees, with many climbing vines and ferns, some of which are a main source of raw materials for medicines.

The rainforest ecosystem helps to regulate global weather patterns – especially by taking up carbon dioxide from the atmosphere – and stabilizes the soil. It provides the bulk of the oxygen needed for plant and animal respiration. When deforestation occurs, the **microclimate** of the mature forest disappears; soil erosion and flooding become major problems since rainforests protect the shallow tropical soils. Once an area is cleared it is very difficult for shrubs and bushes to re-establish because soils are poor in nutrients. This causes problems for plans to convert rainforests into agricul-

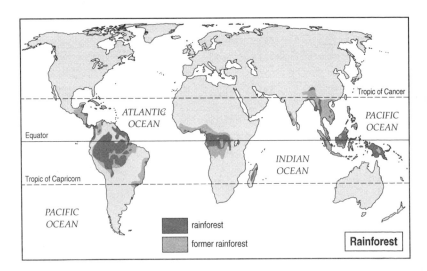

**FACTS ABOUT RAINFORESTS**

▓ Over half the tropical rainforests are in Central and South America. The rest are in southeast Asia, west Africa, and the Congo.

▓ Tropical rainforests are now being destroyed at an increasing rate as their valuable timber is harvested and the land cleared for **agriculture**, causing problems of **deforestation**. They still comprise about 50% of all growing wood on the planet, and harbour at least 40% of the Earth's species (plants and animals).

tural land – after two or three years the crops fail and the land is left bare. Clearing of the rainforests may lead to a global warming of the atmosphere, and contribute to the **greenhouse effect**.

The vegetation in tropical rainforests typically includes:

• selva, an area of dense forest

• a canopy, formed by high branches of tall trees providing shade for lower layers

• an intermediate layer of shorter trees and tree roots

• lianas, climbing plants with stems up to 78 m/255 ft long

• a ground cover of mosses and ferns.

The lack of **seasonal rhythm** causes adjacent plants to flower and shed leaves simultaneously. Chemical **weathering** and leaching take place in the iron-rich soil due to the high temperatures and humidity.

Rainforests comprise some of the most complex and diverse ecosystems on the planet, deriving their energy from the sun and photosynthesis. The trees are the main. Herbivores such as insects, caterpillars, and monkeys feed on the plants and trees and in turn are eaten by the carnivores, such as ocelots and puma. Fungi and bacteria, the primary decomposers, break down the dead material from the plants, herbivores, and carnivores with the help of heat and humidity. This decomposed material provides the nutrients for the plants and trees.

**range**

In physical geography, range means a line of mountains, such as the Alps or Himalayas. In human geography, it means the distance that people are prepared to travel to obtain various goods or services. Range is also a name for an open piece of land where cattle are ranched.

## raw materials

The essential materials and commodities used in industry, before they have been manufactured into goods. Raw materials can include:

- minerals
- skins and fleeces of animals
- timber and fibres
- pig iron
- refined copper.

Raw materials are important economically because some countries are richer in raw materials than others, and because there is increasingly high demand for them from industrialized countries.

## recycling

A way of processing industrial and household waste so that the materials can be reused.

- Paper, glass, and some metals and plastics can be recycled.
- Recycling saves expenditure on scarce raw materials, slows down the depletion of nonrenewable resources, and helps to reduce pollution.
- In 1998 Britain was recycling only 6% of its domestic waste, compared with 25% for the USA, 33% in Japan, and up to 70% in parts of Canada.

  **See also**: *biodegradable.*

## refugee

A person who seeks refuge in a foreign country, after fleeing from oppressive or dangerous conditions such as political, religious, or military persecution. In 1995 there were an estimated 27 million refugees worldwide. Their resettlement and welfare is the responsibility of the United Nations High Commission for Refugees (UNHCR).

- An estimated average of 10,000 people a day become refugees.
- Women and children make up 75% of all refugees and displaced persons.

• Many more millions are 'economic' or 'environmental' refugees, forced to emigrate because of economic circumstances, lack of access to land, or environmental disasters.

## relief
The variations in height of a landscape. An area can be said to have undulating or flat relief. Relief maps show the high and low parts of a particular area.

## renewable energy
Power generated from any source that replenishes itself. Renewable systems rely on:

• **solar power**
• **wave** power
• **hydroelectric** power
• **wind** power via wind turbines
• tidal power
• geothermal energy from the heat trapped deep in the **Earth**.

   **See also**: *energy, alternative; energy resources, renewable resources.*

## renewable resources
Natural resource that is replaced naturally in a reasonable amount of time. **Soil, water, forests**, plants, and animals are all renewable resources as long as they are properly conserved.

   **See also**: *nonrenewable energy.*

## reserves
Stocks of money held back in case of emergency or in order to be used at a later date. Gold bullion and foreign currency reserves are held by a central bank, such as the Bank of England. They are used to intervene in the foreign exchange market in order to change the exchange rate. If the Bank of England buys pounds sterling by selling some of its foreign currency reserves, the value of the pound should rise, and vice versa.

## reservoir
A lake created by people to provide water which may be used for drinking, washing, manufacturing, generating **hydroelectric** power, and irrigation.

---

**PROS AND CONS OF LARGE RESERVOIRS**

▓ Very large open reservoirs contained behind dams are essential if the full potential of a river or river system is to be realized for irrigation, hydroelectric power, and water supply.

▓ Large reservoirs provide suitably high water pressure and can absorb fluctuations in flow so that the system operates steadily.

▓ Reservoirs may provide a degree of valuable flood control, some protection against soil erosion, and a measure of navigation on the rivers they cross.

▓ In arid climates evaporation from large reservoirs can sometimes amount to a significant overall loss of water. At the same time the concentration of salts in the water increases, which can have serious consequences for agriculture.

▓ Medical problems, especially the diseases bilharzia and malaria, are generally worsened along the shorelines of large reservoirs in hot climates.

▓ The greatest defect in all reservoirs is silting, caused by sediment settling as a river's flow is slowed by the reservoir.

---

Wherever possible natural lakes are adapted, but where they do not exist artificial lakes may be created in a natural drainage area by constructing a dam across some portion of a valley.

**See also**: *catchment area.*

### resort
Town catering for **tourism**, such as a coastal town, or alpine resort. Resorts may also have attractive climate or scenery, or historic interest. Often a high proportion of the workforce is engaged in activities associated with tourism, and there may be seasonal unemployment.

### resources
Materials that can be used to provide for human needs. Resources are often categorized into:

• **human resources**, such as labour, supplies, and skills;

• **natural resources**, such as **climate, fossil fuels**, and **water**. Natural resources are divided into **nonrenewable resources** and **renewable resources**.

Demands for resources made by rich nations are causing concern that the present and future demands of industrial societies cannot be sustained for more than a century or two, and that these demands can only be met at the expense of the Third World and the global environment. Other authorities believe that new technologies will emerge, enabling resources that are now of little importance to replace those being exhausted.

**See also**: *energy resources.*

## ria

Long narrow sea **inlet**, usually branching and surrounded by hills. A ria is deeper and wider towards its mouth, unlike a **fiord**. It is formed by the flooding of a river valley due to either a rise in sea level or a lowering of a landmass.

## ribbon lake

Long, narrow **lake** found on the floor of a glacial trough. A ribbon lake often forms in an elongated hollow carved out by a **glacier**, perhaps where it came across a band of weaker rock. Ribbon lakes can also form when water gathers behind a terminal **moraine** or a landslide. The Lake District in the UK has many ribbon lakes, such as Lake Windermere and Coniston Water.

## Richter scale

Scale used to determine the magnitude of an **earthquake** at its epicentre, based on measurement of seismic waves. The magnitude of an earthquake differs from its intensity, measured by the Mercalli scale, which is subjective and varies from place to place for the same earthquake. The scale is named after US seismologist Charles Richter.

An earthquake's magnitude is a function of the total amount of energy released, and each point on the Richter scale represents a thirty-fold increase in energy over the previous point. The greatest earthquake ever recorded, in 1920 in Gansu, China, measured 8.6 on the Richter scale.

## Richter scale

| Magnitude | Relative amount of energy released | Examples | Year |
|---|---|---|---|
| 1 | 1 | | |
| 2 | 3 | | |
| 3 | 960 | | |
| 4 | 30,000 | Carlisle, England (4.7) | 1979 |
| 5 | 920,000 | Wrexham, Wales (5.1) | 1990 |
| 6 | 29,000,000 | San Fernando (CA) (6.5) | 1971 |
| | | northern Armenia (6.8) | 1988 |

## Richter scale (continued)

| | | | |
|---|---|---|---|
| 7 | 890,000,000 | Loma Prieta (CA) (7.1) | 1989 |
| | | Kobe, Japan (7.2) | 1995 |
| | | Rasht, Iran (7.7) | 1990 |
| | | San Francisco (CA) (7.7–7.9)* | 1906 |
| 8 | 28,000,000,000 | Tangshan, China (8.0) | 1976 |
| | | Gansu, China (8.6) | 1920 |
| | | Lisbon, Portugal (8.7) | 1755 |
| 9 | 850,000,000,000 | Prince William Sound (AK) (9.2) | 1964 |

*Richter's original estimate of a magnitude of 8.3 has been revised by two recent studies carried out by the California Institute of Technology and the US Geological Survey.

## rift valley

Valley formed when a block of the **Earth's** crust subsides between two or more parallel faults. Rift valleys are steep-sided and form where the crust is being pulled apart, as at **ocean ridges**, or in the Great Rift Valley of East Africa.

**See also**: *plate tectonics*.

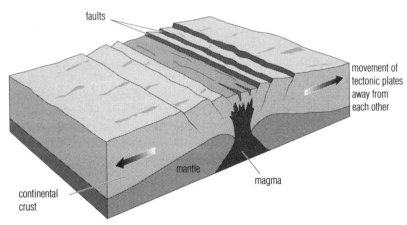

**rift valley** *The formation of a rift valley.*

## river

Large body of water that flows down a slope along a channel restricted by banks. Rivers are formed over time chiefly by **erosion** and by the transport and deposition of **sediment**.

- A river originates at a point called its source, and enters a sea or lake at its mouth.
- Along its length it may be joined by smaller rivers called tributaries.
- A river and its tributaries are contained within a drainage basin.
- The point at which two rivers join is called the **confluence**.
- Major rivers of the world include the Ganges, the Mississippi, and the Nile, the world's longest river.

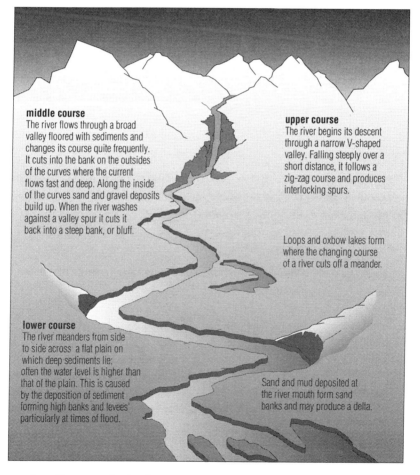

**middle course**
The river flows through a broad valley floored with sediments and changes its course quite frequently. It cuts into the bank on the outsides of the curves where the current flows fast and deep. Along the inside of the curves sand and gravel deposits build up. When the river washes against a valley spur it cuts it back into a steep bank, or bluff.

**upper course**
The river begins its descent through a narrow V-shaped valley. Falling steeply over a short distance, it follows a zig-zag course and produces interlocking spurs.

Loops and oxbow lakes form where the changing course of a river cuts off a meander.

**lower course**
The river meanders from side to side across a flat plain on which deep sediments lie; often the water level is higher than that of the plain. This is caused by the deposition of sediment forming high banks and levees particularly at times of flood.

Sand and mud deposited at the river mouth form sand banks and may produce a delta.

**river** *The course of a river from its source of a spring or melting glacier, through to maturity where it flows into the sea.*

One way of classifying rivers is by their stage of development. A youthful stream is typified by a narrow V-shaped valley with numerous waterfalls, lakes, and rapids. Because of the steep gradient of the topography and the river's height above sea level, the rate of erosion is greater than the rate of deposition and downcutting occurs by vertical **corrasion**. These characteristics may also be said to typify a river's upper course.

In a mature river, the topography has been eroded down over time and the river's course has a shallow gradient. This mature river is said to be graded. Erosion and deposition are delicately balanced as the river meanders (gently curves back and forth) across the extensive flood plain. Horizontal **corrasion** is the dominant erosive process. The flood plain is an area of periodic flooding along the course of river valleys made up of fine silty material called **alluvium** deposited by the flood water. Features of a the mature river (or the lower course of a river) include extensive **meanders**, **oxbow lakes**, and **braiding**.

**See also**: *delta, flood plain, waterfall.*

## road

A route specially constructed for cars, buses, and lorries to travel on. Roads are made from concrete or tarmac.

- Most ancient civilizations had some form of road network.
- The Romans developed engineering techniques for road-building that remained unequalled for 1,400 years.
- Sophisticated construction methods were introduced in the 19th century.
- Recent developments have included durable surface compounds and machinery for preparing the ground rapidly.
- The motorway, or freeway, is the most advanced form of road.

## rock

Hard, solid substance, found on or underneath the **Earth's** crust, and made of consolidated masses of minerals or organic materials. In addition to the mining and extraction of fuels, metals, minerals, and gems, rocks provide useful building and construction materials. Rock is mined through quarrying, and cut into blocks or slabs as building stone, or crushed or broken for other uses in construction work. For instance, cement is made from limestone and, in addition to its use as a bonding material, it can be added to crushed stone, sand, and water to produce strong, durable concrete, which has many applications, such as the construction of roads, runways, and dams.

There are three types of rock:

- **igneous**
- **sedimentary**
- **metamorphic**.

Rocks can often be identified by their location and appearance. For example, sedimentary rocks lie in stratified, or layered, formations and may contain fossils; many have markings such as old mud cracks or ripple marks caused by waves. Except for volcanic glass, all igneous rocks are solid and crystalline. Some appear dense, with microscopic crystals, and others have larger, easily seen crystals. They occur in volcanic areas, and in intrusive formations that geologists call batholiths, laccoliths, sills, dikes, and stocks. Many metamorphic rocks have characteristic bands, and are easily split into sheets or slabs.

Rock formations and **strata** are often apparent in the cliffs that line a seashore, or where rivers have gouged out deep channels to form gorges and canyons. They are also revealed when roads are cut through hillsides, or by excavations for quarrying and mining. Rock and **fossil** collecting has been a popular hobby since the 19th century and such sites can provide a treasure trove of finds for the collector.

**See also**: *clay, limestone, ore, peat, quarry, sandstone, soil, weathering.*

## rotation

The movement of the **Earth** about its own axis, with one complete rotation taking 24 hours. As the Earth's axis is tilted with respect to the Sun, the lengths of day and night vary across the globe.

- At the **Equator**, day and night are both 12 hours long.
- During the northern **hemisphere** winter, days become shorter with increasing latitude north, until a point where there is continuous night.
- At the same time, during the southern hemisphere summer, days become longer with increasing latitude south, until a point where there is continuous daylight.
- The situation is reversed during the northern hemisphere summer.

**See also**: *equinox.*

## run-off

The water that falls as rain and flows over ground, into streams or **rivers**. Run-off occurs when the amount of rainfall exceeds the infiltration capacity of the soil and water cannot be absorbed into rocks or soil.

**See also**: *flood*.

## rural settlement

A place in the countryside such as an isolated dwelling, **hamlet**, or **village**, where people make their homes. Rural settlements may be defined in terms of their distance from **urban** areas, since in densely populated regions it is difficult to distinguish truly rural areas. People who live in rural settlements increasingly suffer from the reduction of services such as public transport, schooling, libraries, and shops.

**See also**: *settlement*.

## salinization
The accumulation of salt in water or soil, making it unusable without treatment to remove some of the salt. Salinization is a factor in **desertification**.

## sand
Loose grains of rock, most commonly made of quartz, but also of other **minerals**. Sand is used in cement-making, as an abrasive, in glass-making, and for other purposes. Some 'light' **soils** contain up to 50% sand. Sands may eventually consolidate into **sandstone**.

## sandstone
**Sedimentary rock** formed from consolidated grains of **sand**. Sandstones are commonly permeable and porous, and may form freshwater **aquifers**. They are mainly used as building materials. (*See illustration on p. 158.*)

## satellite image
An image of the **Earth** or any other planet obtained from instruments on a satellite. Satellite images can provide a variety of information, including vegetation patterns, sea surface temperature, weather, and geology.

- *Landsat 4*, launched in the 1980s, orbits at 705 km/438 mi above the Earth's surface.

- It completes nearly 15 orbits per day, and can survey the entire globe in 16 days.

- The instruments on *Landsat* scan the planet's surface and record the brightness of reflected light (**albedo**).

- The data is transmitted back to Earth and translated into a satellite image.

## savanna
Extensive open tropical grasslands, with scattered trees and shrubs. Savannas cover large areas of Africa, North and South America, and northern Australia. The soil is acidic and sandy and suitable only as pasture for low-density grazing.

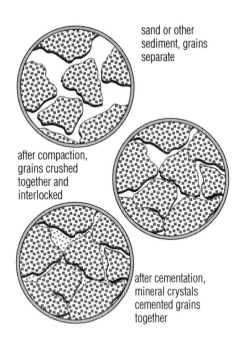

sand or other sediment, grains separate

after compaction, grains crushed together and interlocked

after cementation, mineral crystals cemented grains together

**sandstone** *The formation of sandstone when sand and other sediment grains are compacted and cemented together.*

## scale

The ratio between distances as shown on a map, and as existing in the real world. The scale may be shown by:

• a representative fraction, such as 1:50,000 or 1:25,000

• a scale line

• a statement, such as 'Two centimetres equal one kilometre'.

Scales vary considerably depending on the purpose of the map. The larger the scale, the more detail can be seen of the mapped area. A map with a scale of 1:10,000 may be used for local studies; a typical road atlas has a scale of 1:200,000; and a map of the world will use a scale of 1:80,000,000.

The word 'scale' also refers to the size of an area or process that is being discussed. Principles such as migration, climate, and pollution operate on several scales: local, regional, national, international, and global. It is important to study examples at many different scales.

## scarp and dip

The two slopes which comprise an **escarpment**. The scarp is the steep slope, and the dip is the gentle slope. Scarp and dip is common when **sedimentary rocks** are uplifted, folded, or eroded. The scarp slope cuts across the bedding planes of the sedimentary rock and the dip slope follows the direction of the strata.

**See also**: *erosion*.

## scree

Pile of rubble and **sediment** that collects at the foot of a **mountain** range or **cliff**. The rock fragments that form scree are usually broken off by frost action. In time, the rock waste builds up into a heap or sheet of rubble that may eventually bury even the upper cliffs. Usually, however, the rock waste is eroded so that the scree stays restricted to lower slopes.

**See also**: *erosion*.

## sea

A partially enclosed body of salt water, or a definite part of an **ocean**. Seas may form inland.

**See also**: *tide, wave*.

## seafloor spreading

Sideways spreading and growth of the ocean floor caused by **plate tectonics**. The oceanic plates that form the sea floor move away from the ocean ridges. **Magma** rises up through gaps in the ridge, spreads and solidifies, forming new oceanic crust. The ocean floor thus becomes larger.

## sea-level change

Sea level is the average height of the surface of the oceans and seas. It is affected by:

• a combination of naturally high **tides** and **storm** surge, as sometimes happens along the low-lying coasts of Germany and the Netherlands

• the water walls created by **typhoons** and **hurricanes**, such as often hit Bangladesh

• underwater upheavals in Earth's crust which may cause a **tsunami**

• global temperature change which causes polar ice caps to melt.

Rising sea levels and **erosion** have claimed large portions of the British coastline; particularly along the east coast, where the land has been sinking by half a centimetre per year.

## seamount
Elevation of 1,000 m/3,280 ft or greater above the sea floor. Seamounts are old, extinct submarine volcanoes formed over a **hot spot**. When they occur as linear chains they indicate the motion of a tectonic plate over a hot spot.
   **See also:** *guyot*.

## season
Period of the year having a characteristic **climate**. The change in seasons is mainly due to the change in position of the Earth's axis in relation to the Sun, which affects the position of the Sun in the sky at a particular place.

- In temperate latitudes four seasons are recognized: spring, summer, autumn (fall), and winter.

- Tropical regions have two seasons – the wet and the dry.

- Monsoon areas around the **Indian Ocean** have three seasons: the cold, the hot, and the rainy.

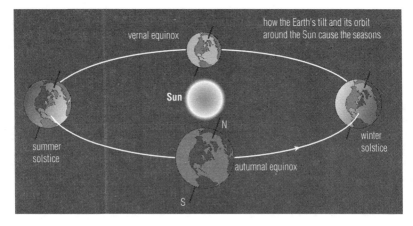

**season** *The cause of the seasons. As the Earth orbits the Sun, its axis always points in the same direction. This affects the position of the Sun in the sky at a particular place, according to the time of year.*

---

**FACTS ABOUT THE SEASONS**

▦ It is summer in the northern temperate latitudes when it is winter in the southern temperate latitudes, and vice versa.

▦ The differences between the seasons are more marked inland than near the coast, where the sea has a moderating effect on temperatures.

▦ In polar regions the change between summer and winter is abrupt; spring and autumn are hardly perceivable.

---

## sediment

Any loose material that settles after being deposited by water, ice, or air. Typical sediments are **clay**, mud, silt, **sand**, gravel, pebbles, cobbles, and boulders.

**See also**: *sedimentary rock*.

## sedimentary rock

**Rock** formed by the consolidation of **sediment**. Pebbles are consolidated into conglomerates; sands become **sandstones**; muds become mudstones or shales; **peat** is transformed into **coal**. Sedimentary rocks cover more than two-thirds of the **Earth's** surface. Non-organic sedimentary rocks are made up of particles of older rocks which have been eroded and then deposited again by wind, water, or ice. As such, they can reveal a lot about past environments.

- Clastic sediments are the largest group and are composed of fragments of pre-existing rocks; they include clays, sands, and gravels.

- Chemically precipitated sediments include some **limestones** and evaporated deposits such as gypsum and halite (rock salt).

- Organic sedimentary rocks include **coal**, oil shale, and limestone made of **fossil** material.

Most sedimentary rocks show distinct strata, caused by alterations in composition or by changes in rock type. These strata may become folded or fractured by the movement of the Earth's crust.

## settlement

Place where people live, varying in size from isolated dwellings to the largest cities. Most owe their origin to historical and geographical factors.

Many present-day towns and cities were originally based on a specific function such as mining. As the settlement evolved, it took on other functions, sometimes developing into a vast urbanized area.

**See also**: *city, hamlet, rural settlement, shanty town, urban, village.*

## sewage

All waterborne waste products from houses, streets, and factories, including human waste. Conveyed through sewers to sewage works, sewage undegoes a series of treatments before it is discharged into rivers or the sea. In most countries, sewage works for residential areas are the responsibility of local authorities. The solid waste (sludge) may be spread over fields as a **fertilizer** or, in a few countries, dumped at sea. Raw sewage, or sewage that has not been treated adequately, is one serious source of **water pollution** and a cause of **eutrophication**.

## shanty town

Group of shelters constructed from cheap or waste materials, such as cardboard and wood, found in poor countries and usually located on derelict land, near rubbish tips, or on the outskirts of **cities**. Shanty areas are crowded, and often lack running water, electricity, and sanitation. Shanty towns result from mass **migration** from rural areas as people move to cities in search for jobs.

## shifting cultivation

System where farmers move from one place to another when the land becomes exhausted. The most common form is slash-and-burn **agriculture**, practised in many tropical forest areas, such as the Amazon region, where land is cleared by burning so that crops can be grown. After a few years, soil fertility is reduced, the land is abandoned, and a new area is cleared while the old land recovers its fertility. This system works well while population levels are low, but where there is **overpopulation**, the old land has to be reused before soil fertility has been restored.

## shingle

A mixture of pebbles and gravel, worn by water and found on the higher parts of beaches. Shingle is deposited on beaches by large **waves** during **storms**. It accumulates into ridges, because it is too heavy to be transported by normal waves.

**See also**: *spit.*

## slate

Fine-grained **metamorphic rock**, usually grey, that splits easily into thin slabs. Slate is highly resistant to atmospheric conditions and can be written on with chalk (actually gypsum). It takes such skill and time to **quarry** slate that it is now seldom used for roof and sill material except in restoring historic buildings.

## slum

Area of poor-quality housing, usually found in the inner **city** in rich countries and in older parts of cities in poor countries. Slum housing is densely populated, in a bad state of repair, and has inadequate services such as sanitation. Its occupants are often poor with low rates of literacy. The clearing of slum areas has often been a priority in **urban** redevelopment.

## smallholding

A small farm, where a few crops are grown and animals raised for sale to local people. A smallholding may be run by a single family with no additional labour force.

**See also**: *agriculture*.

## smog

Natural **fog** containing impurities from domestic fires, industrial furnaces, power stations, and traffic exhaust fumes. Smog can damage wildlife and cause illness and loss of life. The use of smokeless fuels, the treatment of effluent, and penalties for excessive smoke from poorly maintained and operated vehicles can be effective in reducing smog, but it still occurs in many cities throughout the world.

## snow

Soft, white, crystalline flakes which fall from the **atmosphere** and are caused by the condensation of excess water vapour on to ice crystals in a **cloud**. Light reflecting in the crystals gives snow its white appearance. Snow seldom falls unless the air temperature is below 4°C/39°F. Heavy snowfalls are usually associated with active **fronts**.

## soil

Loose material formed of broken rock and decaying organic matter that lies on much of the **Earth's** surface, and in which plants can grow. Soil contains minerals, organic matter, living organisms, air, and water.

A soil can be described in terms of its soil profile, a vertical cross-section from ground-level to the bedrock on which the soils sits. The profile is divided into layers called horizons.

- The A horizon, or topsoil, is the uppermost layer, consisting primarily of humus, living organisms, and mineral material. Most soluble material has been leached from this layer or washed down to the B horizon.

To remember the chief constituents of soil:
**A**ll **h**airy **m**en **w**ill **b**uy **r**azors
**Air, humus, mineral salts, water, bacteria, rock particles**

A handful of soil contains up to 5,000 species of bacteria.

- The B horizon, or subsoil, is the layer where most of the nutrients accumulate and is enriched in clay minerals.
- The C horizon is the layer of weathered material at the base of the soil.

The organic content of soil is widely variable, ranging from zero in some desert soils to almost 100% in peats. Soils influence **agriculture**. Light, well-drained soils favour **arable** farming, whereas heavy clay soils give rise to lush pasture land.

## soil erosion
The wearing away and redistribution of the Earth's layer of soil, caused by water, wind, and ice, and also by poor agricultural practices. If unchecked, soil erosion results in desertification.

### FACTS ABOUT SOIL EROSION

- If the rate of erosion exceeds the rate of soil formation, the land will become infertile.
- **Deforestation** often leads to serious soil erosion, because plant roots bind soil, and without them the soil is free to wash or blow away. The effect is worse on hillsides.
- Improved agricultural practices such as contour ploughing are needed to combat soil erosion. Planting windbreaks, such as hedges or strips of coarse grass, is valuable, and organic farming can reduce soil erosion by as much as 75%.
- Soil degradation and erosion are becoming as serious as the loss of **rainforest**. Around 20% of the world's cultivated topsoil was lost between 1950 and 1990.

## solar power

Power derived by harnessing energy from the Sun's radiation. The amount of energy falling on just 1 sq km is about 4,000 megawatts, enough to heat and light a small town. Although it is difficult to generate a high output from solar energy compared to sources such as **nuclear** or **fossil fuels**, it is a major non-polluting and **renewable energy** source. A number of solar-energy technologies have emerged during recent years.

- **Solar heaters** have industrial or domestic uses. They usually consist of a black, heat-absorbing panel containing pipes through which air or water, heated by the Sun, is circulated, either by thermal convection or by a pump.

- Solar energy may also be harnessed indirectly using **solar cells** made of panels that generate electricity when illuminated by sunlight.

## solar radiation

Radiation given off by the Sun, consisting mainly of visible light, ultraviolet, and infrared.

## solstice

Time when the Sun is furthest from the **Equator**. In the northern hemisphere the summer solstice occurs on about 21 June, when the Sun is furthest north from the Equator and is directly overhead at the Tropic of Cancer. At the winter solstice, 22 December the Sun is at its furthest south from the Equator and is directly overhead at the Tropic of Capricorn.

## South America

South America, fourth largest continent in the world and connected to North America by the isthmus of Panama, is made up of 13 countries of which Brazil is the largest. Half the continent's total population of 300 million people live in Brazil. South America supports an extraordinary diversity of animals. This is partly because for millions of years it was separated by sea from North America, and so animals could thrive without threat from the north. Another factor is the South American geography in which equatorial **rainforest** and Alpine **tundra**, lowland pampas, searing **deserts** and snow-capped **mountain** ranges lie in close proximity. Animals found in South America include tapirs, vicuna, many species of monkey, and the sloth. A quarter of all bird species live in South America. Fur-bearing animals have been severely depleted by commercial hunters. Many habitats have been lost by the intensive development of the pampas for ranching and exploitation of the rainforest.

The Andes are an extensive chain of mountains which stretch the length of the continent, and at 7,200 km/4,474 mi are the world's longest range. Lake Titicaca, the world's highest navigable lake, lies in the mountains, at 3,800 m/12,468 ft. The basin of the Amazon, the world's largest and second longest river, is a huge lowland area containing the largest rainforest in the world. All the species living here are considered to be endangered, because so much of the forest is being lost to make farmland. The vast Patagonian plateau in the south consists of pampas grasslands where wheat is grown and cattle raised on ranches.

South America produces:

- coffee and cocoa
- citrus fruit, bananas, mangoes
- tobacco
- meat
- soya beans
- cotton, linseed, sunflower seed
- tin, manganese, silver, and copper.

## spit

Ridge of **sand** or **shingle** projecting from the land into a body of water. It is

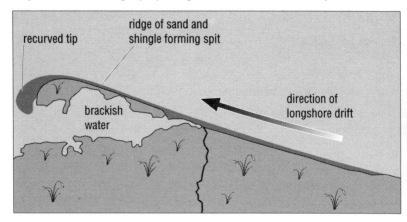

**spit**  *Spits form when longshore drift, carrying sand and shingle along coastlines, is interrupted. Deposited material gradually builds up forming a new stretch of land called a spit. A spit that extends a cross a bay is called a bar.*

formed by the interruption of **longshore drift** when tides, currents, or a bend in the coastline reduce wave energy. This means that more material is deposited, and a finger or ridge builds up pointing in the direction of the longshore drift.

## spring

A natural flow of water from the ground, formed where the water table meets the ground's surface. The source of water is rain that has percolated through the overlying rocks. During its underground passage, the water may acquire dissolved mineral substances. A spring may be continuous or intermittent, depending on the position of the water table and the topography.

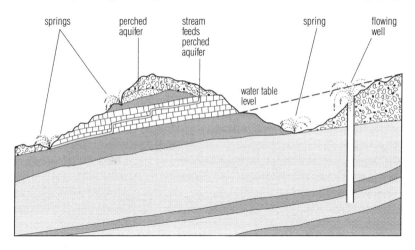

**spring** *Springs occur where aquifers reach the surface. Water will flow from a well whose head is below the water table.*

## spur

Ridge of rock jutting out into a valley or plain. In mountainous areas **rivers** often flow around interlocking spurs because they are not powerful enough to erode through the spurs. Spurs may be eroded by **glaciers** to form truncated spurs.

**See also**: *erosion*.

## stack

Isolated pillar of **rock** that has become separated from a headland by **coastal erosion**. It is usually formed when an **arch** collapses. Further erosion will reduce it to a stump, which is exposed only at low tide. Examples of stacks are the chalk Needles, off the Isle of Wight in the UK.

### stalactite
Pendants found in **caves**, formed by deposits of calcite dissolved in **groundwater**. Stalactites and **stalagmites** may meet to form a continuous column from floor to ceiling. Stalactites grow downwards from the roofs or walls and can be icicle-shaped, straw-shaped, curtain-shaped, or formed as terraces. They are formed when groundwater, hanging as a drip, deposits a small trace of calcite. Successive drips build up the stalactite over many years.

### stalagmite
Pillars found in **caves**, formed when calcite comes out of solution in **groundwater** because of agitation – the shock of a drop of water hitting the floor is sufficient to remove some calcite from the drop. Stalagmites grow upwards from the cave floor and can be conical, fir-cone-shaped, or resemble a stack of saucers. In stalagmite formation the different shapes result from the splashing of the falling water.
**See also**: *stalactite.*

### steppe
The huge areas of temperate **grasslands** found in Europe and Asia. They have been altered by cultivation and excessive grazing by livestock.
**See also**: *prairie.*

### storm
Any strong wind, particularly one accompanied by heavy **rain, snow, hail**, or **dust**. A wind force of 10 on the **Beaufort scale** constitutes a storm. A storm surge is an abnormally high tide which can cause severe **flooding** of lowland coastal regions and river **estuaries**.
**See also**: *thunderstorm.*

### subsidence
The downward movement of a block of rock. Subsidence is usually due to the removal of material from below the surface, and can be caused by faults, erosion, or by human activities such as mining.

### subsistence farming
A type of farming that produces only enough to feed the farmer and family, with no surplus to sell.

## suburb

Outer part of a city or town, consisting of residential housing and small shops. The growth of suburbs may result in **urban** sprawl.

## sustainable development

Development that meets present needs without compromising the ability of future generations to meet their own needs. The term is often used to refer to the goals of economic development, but also embraces social, cultural, and environmental activities.

## swamp

Region of low-lying land that is permanently saturated with water and usually overgrown with vegetation; for example, the everglades of Florida, USA. A swamp often occurs where a lake has filled up with **sediment** and plant material. The flat surface formed in this way means that **run-off** is slow, and the **water table** is always close to the surface. The high humus content of swamp land means that good agricultural soil can be obtained by draining.

## swash

The movement of water and **sediment** up a **beach** as a **wave** breaks. Swash plays a significant role in **longshore drift**, and is responsible for throwing **shingle** and pebbles up a beach.

**See also**: *backwash, coastal erosion, spit.*

## taiga or boreal forest

Dense forest of conifers and poplars occupying **glaciated** northern regions south of the **tundra**. The forests are punctuated with cold **lakes**, streams, **bogs**, and **marshes**. Winters are prolonged and very cold, but the summer is warm enough to promote dense growth. The varied fauna and flora are in delicate balance because the conditions of life are so precarious. This ecology is threatened by **mining, forestry**, and pipeline construction.

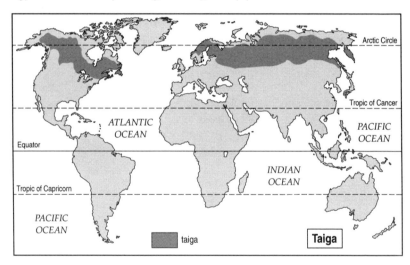

taiga

**Taiga**

## teleworking

A method of working from home rather than in an office, using a telephone and a personal computer connected to the office via a modem. Convenient for employers as it reduces overheads, teleworking also makes part-time working easier for those with other commitments, such as young children. However, it has proved more costly to administer than many advocates had anticipated in the 1980s.

• Teleworking is most successful when combined with some attendance at the workplace.

- In 1991 an estimated 500,000 people in Britain were employed full time in this way, with a further 1.5 million part-time.
- According to a 1997 estimate, about 2% of the US population were tele-working on any given day.

## temperate deciduous forest
A type of vegetation mass, covering over 4.5% of the **Earth's** land surface and found mainly in **Europe**, the USA, and China. Common tree species are oak, maple, and beech and the annual leaf fall means that soils are rich in nutrients.

- The overall area of temperate deciduous forest has declined rapidly since the **agricultural revolution**.
- In western Europe reafforestation schemes are gradually leading to the expansion of forest area.

**See also**: *deforestation.*

## temperate grasslands
A vegetation type, dominated by deep rooted native grasses, found in areas with a dry **continental climate** with a summer drought. Temperate grass-lands cover 6% of the Earth's land surface and are found in the USA (**prairies**), central **Asia** (**steppe**) and **South America** (pampas)

## Third World
The undeveloped countries of the world, now more often referred to as developing countries. The name comes from a UN classification, under which the industrialized free-market countries of the west were the First World, the industrialized former Communist countries the Second World. Third World countries are the poorest, as measured by their income per head of population, and are concentrated in Asia, Africa, and Latin America.

Despite enormous differences in history, geography, social structure, and culture, Third World countries have the following characteristics in common:

- their modern industrial sectors are relatively undeveloped
- they are mainly producers of primary commodities for the western indus-trialized countries, for which prices and demand fluctuate
- their populations are poor and chiefly engaged in agriculture

- they have high population growth and mortality rates; poor educational and health facilities; high levels of underemployment; and, in some cases, political instability.

Failure by many developing countries to meet their enormous foreign **debt** obligations has led to stringent terms being imposed on loans by industrialized countries

### terraces

Large steps cut into a slope to provide level land suitable for farming. The terraces may be edged with low walls to help retain moisture and prevent **soil** creep.

### terracettes

Tiny steps on a hillside, formed by **soil** creep, when soil moves slowly, but continuously down a slope.

### thunderstorm

Severe storm including very heavy **rain**, thunder, and lightning. Thunderstorms are usually caused by the intense heating of the ground surface during summer. The warm air rises rapidly to form tall cumulonimbus **clouds** with a characteristic anvil-shaped top. Electrical charges accumulate in the clouds and are discharged to the ground as flashes of lightning. Air in the path of lightning becomes heated and expands rapidly, creating shock waves that are heard as a crash or rumble of thunder.

The rough distance between an observer and a lightning flash can be calculated by timing the number of seconds between the flash and the thunder. A gap of three seconds represents about a kilometre; five seconds represents about a mile.

**See also**: *storm*.

### tide

The rhythmic rise and fall of the **sea** level in the **oceans** and their inlets and estuaries. Tides are due to the gravitational attraction of the Moon and, to a lesser extent, the Sun, affecting areas unequally as it rotates.

- High tide occurs at intervals of 12 hr 24 min 30 sec.
- The maximum high tides, or spring tides, occur at or near new and full Moon when the Moon and Sun are in line and exert the greatest combined gravitational pull.

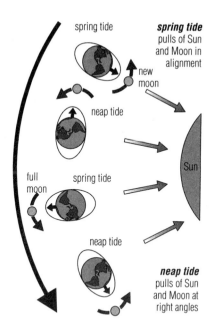

spring tide

**spring tide**
pulls of Sun
and Moon in
alignment

new
moon

neap tide

Sun

full
moon

spring tide

neap tide

**neap tide**
pulls of Sun
and Moon at
right angles

**tide** *The gravitational pull of the Moon is the main cause of the tides. Water on the side of the Earth nearest the Moon feels the Moon's pull and accumulates directly under the Moon. When the Sun and the Moon are in line, at new and full moon, the gravitational pull of Sun and Moon are in line and produce a high spring tide. When the Sun and Moon are at right angles, lower neap tides occur.*

- Lower high tides, or neap tides, occur when the Moon is in its first or third quarter and the Moon and Sun are at right angles to each other.

## timber

Wood used in construction, furniture, and the manufacture of paper pulp.

- **Hardwoods** include tropical mahogany, teak, ebony, rosewood, temperate oak, elm, beech, and eucalyptus. All except eucalyptus are slow-growing, and world supplies are almost exhausted.

- **Softwoods** comprise the conifers (pine, fir, spruce, and larch), which are quick to grow and easy to work but inferior in quality of grain.

- **White woods** include ash, birch, and sycamore; all have light-coloured timber, are fast-growing, and can be used as veneers on cheaper timber.

## topography

The surface shape and composition of the landscape, including both natural and artificial features. Topographical features include the **relief** and **contours** of the land; the distribution of **mountains**, **valleys**, and human **settlements**; and the patterns of **rivers**, **roads**, and **railways**.

**See also**: *landmark, maps.*

## topsoil

The upper, cultivated layer of **soil**, which may vary in depth from 8–45 cm/ 3–18 in. It contains the decayed remains of vegetation, which plants need for active growth, along with a variety of soil organisms, including earthworms.

## tor

Isolated mass of **rock**, often **granite**, left on a hilltop after the surrounding rock has been broken down. **Weathering** takes place along the joints in the rock, reducing it to a mass of rounded blocks.

## tornado

Extremely violent revolving **storm** with swirling, funnel-shaped clouds, caused by a rising column of warm air propelled by strong wind. A tornado can rise to a great height, but have a diameter of only a few hundred metres or less.

A series of tornadoes killed 47 people, destroyed 2,000 homes, and caused $500 million worth of damage in Oklahoma, Nebraska, Kansas, and Texas in May 1999.

Tornadoes move with wind speeds of 160–480 kph/100–300 mph, destroying everything in their path. They are common in central USA and Australia.

**See also**: *hurricane, storm, whirlwind, wind.*

## tourism

Industry providing travellers with travel, tours, overnight accommodation, meals and entertainment. Tourism can increase the wealth and job opportunities in an area, although the work is often seasonal and low paid. Among the negative effects of tourism are traffic congestion and overcrowding, as well as damage to the environment.

- Tourism is the world's largest industry. It sustained 120 million jobs in 1995, accounting for 7% of the global workforce.

- It is estimated that the number of international travellers in 1994 will double, to reach 1 billion by 2010.
- 80% of tourists come from the 20 richest countries.
  **See also**: *resort.*

## town
Settlement larger than a **village** and smaller than a **city**. Towns typically have a population of 4,000–90,000. A town may be dominated by one function; for example, an industrial town or a resort town.

## trade
The exchange of commodities between groups, individuals, or countries. Direct trade, where commodities themselves are exchanged, is called barter. Indirect trade is carried on using money to pay for goods.

---

### FACTS ABOUT TRADE

■ International trade patterns have evolved out of the relationships between European and North American countries and their former colonies.

■ Less economically developed countries in South America, Asia, and Africa supply raw materials to more economically developed countries for manufacturing into goods. After going through the manufacturing process, the raw materials become more valuable.

■ Efforts to improve the economy of poorer countries focus on the development of a manufacturing sector.

---

## trade winds
Prevailing **winds** that blow towards the **equator** from the northeast and southeast. Trade winds are caused when hot air rises at the equator and air from north and south moves to take its place. The winds are deflected towards the west because of the Earth's west-to-east rotation. The trade-wind belts move north and south about 5° with the seasons. The unpredictable calms known as the doldrums lie where the trade winds converge.

## transhumanance
The movement of dairy cattle in the Alps between mountain pastures in the summer, and valley pastures in the winter.

## transpiration
The process by which leaves give off water vapour. With **evaporation** it forms the means by which **water** moves from the **Earth's** surface to the **atmosphere** in the **hydrological cycle**. Transpiration is most significant over forest areas, and **deforestation** can result in the local **climate** becoming less humid.

## transport
The moving of people or goods from one place to another.

---

**FACTS ABOUT TRANSPORT**

■ With the development of the steam engine during the **industrial revolution**, horse transport began to be replaced by **railways**.

■ At the beginning of the 20th century, transport methods making use of the internal combustion engine began to be developed, and gradually **road** transport by car, van, and lorry superseded use of the horse.

■ The bicycle, as a nonpolluting method of personal transport, has become popular again in the latter half of the 20th century.

■ The use of steamships for water transport was widespread by the end of the 19th century.

■ In the early 20th century, aircraft began to be developed and were produced commercially after the First World War.

---

## treeline
The highest point on a **mountain** where trees will grow, and above which it is too cold for them to survive.

## tributary
**River** or stream that joins a larger river. For example, the River Teme is a tributary of the River Severn.

## tropical rainforest
See *rainforest*.

## Tropics

The area north and south of the equator which lies between between the parallels of latitude known as the tropics of Cancer and Capricorn. These mark the limits of the area in which the Sun can be directly overhead. The average monthly temperature of the Tropics is over 20°C/68°F. Climates within the tropics lie in parallel bands:

- Along the equator is the intertropical convergence zone, characterized by high temperatures and year-round heavy rainfall. **Tropical rainforests** are found here.

- Along the tropics themselves lie the tropical high-pressure zones, characterized by descending dry air and desert conditions.

- Between these zones, the conditions vary seasonally between wet and dry, producing the tropical grasslands.

### tsunami

A long, **high ocean** wave caused by **earthquakes** or **volcanic** activity on the sea floor. Unlike waves generated by surface winds, the entire depth of water is involved in the wave motion. In the coastal shallows tsunamis slow down and build up producing huge swells over 15 m/45 ft high. Before each wave there may be a sudden withdrawal of water from the beach. The waves sweep inland causing great loss of life and property. On 26 May 1983, an earthquake in the Pacific Ocean caused tsunamis up to 14 m/42 ft high, which killed 104 people along the west coast of Japan near Minehama, Honshu.

### tundra

A huge, flat, **arctic** region of **permafrost**, devoid of trees, and with characteristic vegetation of grasses, sedges, heather, mosses, and lichens. Tundra stretches in a continuous belt across northern North America and Eurasia. (*See map on p. 178.*)

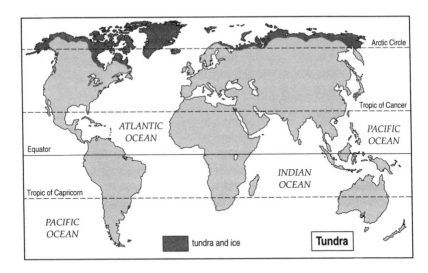

tundra and ice

Tundra

## typhoon
A violent revolving storm, occurring in the western **Pacific Ocean**. It may also be known as a **hurricane**, or a **cyclone**.

## United Nations (UN)

International organization established in 1945, to promote peace, security, and cooperation. It was established in 1945 by 51 states as a successor to the League of Nations, and has played a role in many areas, such as refugees, development assistance, disaster relief, cultural cooperation, and peacekeeping. Its headquarters are in New York City.

- UN membership in 1996 stood at 185 states, and the total proposed budget for 1995–96 (raised by the member states) was $2,600 million supporting more than 50,000 staff.

- The principal UN institutions are the General Assembly, the Security Council, the Economic and Social Council, the Trusteeship Council, all based in New York; and the International Court of Justice in The Hague, Netherlands.

- In its peacekeeping role, acting in pursuance of Security Council resolutions, the UN has had mixed success. The number of peacekeeping operations increased from 1 during 1975–85, to 25 during 1985–95.

- The UN has always suffered from a lack of adequate and independent funds and forces. In 1996, owed $3 billion by its members (two-thirds by the USA and Russia), the UN was forced to slash programmes and reduce staffing.

## urban

To do with a town or **city**. Around one-third of the world's population live in urban **settlements** with a population over 20,000, and this percentage is increasing due to a growth in urbanization.

## urbanization

The process by which the proportion of a population living in or around towns and cities increases, as the agricultural population decreases. The growth or urban centres in the USA and Europe dates back to the start of the **industrial revolution**. It is predicted that by 2006 the majority of the world's population will be living in urban conglomerations. Almost all urban growth will occur in the developing world, spawning ten large cities per year. Urbanization has had a major effect on the social structures of industrial societies, affecting not only where people live but how they live.

## Highest and lowest urban populations, 1997

| Rank | Country | Population living in urban areas (%) |
|------|---------|--------------------------------------|
| *Highest Urban Population* | | |
| 1 | Vatican City State | 100* |
| 2 | Monaco | 100 |
| 3 | Nauru | 100 |
| 4 | Singapore | 100 |
| 5 | Belgium | 97 |
| 6 | Kuwait | 97 |
| 7 | Andorra | 95 |
| 8 | San Marino | 95 |
| 9 | Iceland | 92 |
| 10 | Qatar | 92 |
| *Lowest Urban Population* | | |
| 1 | Rwanda | 6 |
| 2 | Bhutan | 7 |
| 3 | Burundi | 8 |
| 4 | Nepal | 11 |
| 5 | Uganda | 13 |
| 6 | Malawi | 14 |
| 7 | Burkina Faso | 17 |
| 8 | Ethiopia | 17 |
| 9 | Papua New Guinea | 17 |
| 10 | Eritrea | 18 |

*1995.

*Source*: World Health Organization.

## valley

A long stretch of low land, lying between hills. Usually a stream or **river** runs along the floor of a valley. **Mountain** valleys may be steep-sided, with little or no flat land on either side of their rivers. Lowland valleys may have gently sloping sides, and large areas of meadow flanking their rivers.

**See also**: *canyon, dry valley, glacier and glaciation, gully, rift valley, wadi.*

## vegetation

The plant life of a particular area, such as shrubs, trees, and bushes. The type of vegetation depends on:

- the **soil**, which may become impoverished by **deforestation**;
- **climate**, especially the amount of moisture available and the possibility of frost, since these influence the types of vegetation that can survive;
- human activity, such as overgrazing and destruction of **grasslands**.

**See also**: *biome.*

## village

**Rural settlement** larger than a **hamlet**, and smaller than a **town**, with a population of 200–3,000. Although the primary function of villages is residential, they may contain a church, a pub, and perhaps a post office and general store.

## volcano

A mountain or hill on which there are cracks in the **Earth's** crust through which molten rock, called **magma**, and gases well up. The magma is called **lava** when it reaches the surface. A volcanic mountain, usually cone shaped with a crater on top, is formed around the opening, or vent, by the build-up of solidified lava and ash. Most volcanoes arise on plate margins (see **plate tectonics**), where the movements of plates generate magma or allow it to rise from the **mantle** beneath. However, a number are found far from plate-margin activity, on 'hot spots' where the Earth's crust is thin. The islands of Hawaii are an example.

Many volcanoes are submarine and occur along mid-ocean ridges. The chief terrestrial volcanic regions are around the Pacific rim, the central Andes of Chile, North Island, New Zealand, Hawaii, Japan, and Antarctica. There are more than 1,300 potentially active volcanoes.

---

**STAGES IN THE LIFE OF A VOLCANO**

■ The first stages of an eruption are usually vigorous as the magma forces its way to the surface.

■ As the pressure drops and the vents become established, the main phase of activity begins.

■ When the pressure from below ceases, due to exhaustion of the magma chamber, activity wanes and is confined to the emission of gases. In time this also ceases. The volcano then enters a period of quiescence, after which activity may resume after a period of days, years, or even thousands of years.

■ Only when the root zones of a volcano have been exposed by erosion can a volcano be said to be truly extinct.

---

There are two types of volcano: composite and shield. Composite volcanoes, such as Stromboli and Vesuvius in Italy, are found at destructive plate margins - areas where plates are being pushed together - usually in association with island arcs and coastal mountain chains. The magma is mostly derived from continental plate material and is rich in silica. This makes a very stiff lava such as andesite, which solidifies rapidly to form a high, steep-sided volcanic mountain. The magma often clogs the volcanic vent, causing violent eruptions as the blockage is blasted free, as in the eruption of Mount St Helens, USA, in 1980. The crater may collapse to form a caldera.

Mt. Pelée volcanoe erupted in Martinique in 1902. All but one of the port of Saint Pierre's 30,000 inhabitants were killed by the force of the eruption, the survivor was protected by the thick walls of his jail cell.

The dangers of an explosive volcano

• *Pyroclastics* Fragments of solidified volcanic magma, ranging in size from fine ash to large boulders are ejected during an explosive volcanic

composite
volcano

cinder
cone

shield volcano

**volcano** *There are two main types of volcano, but three distinctive cone shapes. Composite volcanoes such as Vesuvius in Italy, emit a stiff lava, rapidly solidifying lava which forms high, steep-sided cones. Volcanoes that regularly throw out ash build up flatter domes, known as cinder cones. The lava from a shield volcano, such as Mauna Loa in Hawaii, is free-flowing, which is not ejected violently, but flows over the crater rim forming a broad, low volcano.*

eruption. Pyroclastic rocks include tuff, which forms from welded ash and volcanic breccia.

- *Lahar* During a volcanic eruption, melting ice may combine with ash to form a powerful mud flow capable of causing great destruction. The lahars created by the eruption of Nevado del Ruiz in Colombia, South America, in 1985 buried 22,000 people in 8 m/26 ft of mud.

- *Nuée ardente* A nuée ardente is a rapidly flowing, glowing white-hot cloud of ash and gas emitted during a violent eruption. The ash and other pyroclastics in the lower part of the cloud behave like an ash flow. In 1902 a nuée ardente produced by the eruption of Mount Pelee in Martinique swept down the volcano in a matter of seconds and killed 28,000 people in the nearby town of St Pierre.

The lava of a shield volcano is not ejected violently but simply flows over the crater rim. Shield volcanoes, such as Mauna Loa in

Hawaii, are found along the rift valleys and ocean ridges of constructive plate margins and also over hot spots. The magma is derived from the Earth's mantle and is quite free-flowing. The lava formed from this magma – usually basalt – flows for some distance over the surface before it sets and so forms broad low volcanoes.

## Major volcanic eruptions since 1985

| Volcano | Location | Year | Estimated number of deaths |
|---|---|---|---|
| Nevado del Ruiz | Colombia | 1985 | 23,000 |
| Lake Nyos | Cameroon | 1986 | 1,700 |
| Pinatubo | Luzon, Philippines | 1991 | 639 |
| Unzen | Japan | 1991 | 39 |
| Mayon | Philippines | 1993 | 70 |
| Loki* | Iceland | 1996 | 0 |
| Soufriere | Montserrat | 1997 | 23 |
| Merapi | Java, Indonesia | 1998 | 38 |

*The eruption caused severe flooding, and melted enough ice to create a huge sub-glacial lake.

## wadi
A steep-sided **valley** found in arid regions of the Middle East, containing a stream that flows only in the wet season.

## waste disposal
The disposal of waste material such as household rubbish, **sewage**, and waste from industry. Methods of waste disposal include incineration, burial at designated sites, and dumping at sea.

---

### WASTE DISPOSAL AND THE ENVIRONMENT

■ Nuclear waste and toxic waste are usually buried or dumped at sea, although this does not negate the danger.

■ Environmental groups, such as Greenpeace and Friends of the Earth, are campaigning for more recycling, production of fewer packaging materials, and safer methods of disposal.

■ Although incineration cuts down on landfill and can produce heat as a useful by-product, it is still a wasteful method of disposal in comparison with recycling. For example, recycling a plastic bottle saves twice as much energy as is obtained by burning it.

---

**See also**: *pollution, nonrenewable resources, water pollution.*

## water cycle
**See** *hydrological cycle.*

## waterfall
A place where a **river** or stream flows over a steep drop. Waterfalls develop when a river flows over a bed of rock that resists **erosion**. Softer rocks downstream are worn away, creating a vertical drop and a plunge pool into which the water falls. Over time, continuing erosion causes the waterfall to retreat upstream forming a deep **valley**, or **gorge**. (*See illustration on p. 186.*)

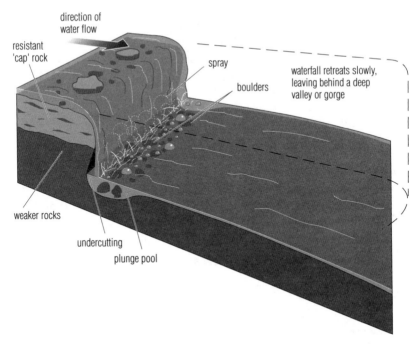

**waterfall** *When water flows over hard and soft rock, the soft rocks erode, creating waterfalls. As the erosion continues, the falls move backwards, in the opposite direction to the water flow.*

## Ten highest waterfalls in the world

| Waterfall | Location | Total drop | |
|---|---|---|---|
| | | m | ft |
| Angel Falls | Venezuela | 979 | 3,212 |
| Yosemite Falls | USA | 739 | 2,425 |
| Mardalsfossen–South | Norway | 655 | 2,149 |
| Tugela Falls | South Africa | 614 | 2,014 |
| Cuquenan | Venezuela | 610 | 2,000 |
| Sutherland | New Zealand | 580 | 1,903 |
| Ribbon Fall, Yosemite | USA | 491 | 1,612 |
| Great Karamang River Falls | Guyana | 488 | 1,600 |
| Mardalsfossen–North | Norway | 468 | 1,535 |
| Della Falls | Canada | 440 | 1,443 |

### water pollution
The contamination of fresh or sea water so that biological processes are damaged, or a health hazard caused. Common pollutants include nitrates, pesticides, and **sewage**, although a huge range of industrial contaminants – such as chemical by-products and residues created in the manufacture of various goods – also enter water legally, accidentally, and through illegal dumping.
    **See also**: *pollution, waste disposal.*

### watershed
A ridge of high land from which rainwater will flow into a **river**. It marks the boundary of that river's **drainage** basin. A watershed may run along a mountain ridge, and be the dividing line between two drainage basins, one on each side of the ridge.

### waterspout
Funnel-shaped column of water and cloud that is drawn from the surface of the **sea** or a **lake** by a **tornado**.

### water table
The upper level of **groundwater**, below which the ground is saturated with water. Water above the water table will drain downwards. **Springs** form where the water table meets the surface of the ground. The water table rises and falls in response to rainfall and the rate at which water is extracted, for example, for irrigation and industry.
    In many irrigated areas the water table is falling due to the extraction of water. Regions with high water tables and dense industrialization have problems with **pollution** of the water table. In the USA, some states have water tables contaminated by both industrial wastes and saline seepage from the **ocean**.

### wave
A ridge or swell of water in a **lake** or **sea**, formed by wind or other causes. The power of a wave is determined by the strength of the wind and the distance of open water over which the wind blows. Waves are the main cause of **coastal erosion** and **deposition** – sweeping away or building up **beaches**, creating **spits**, and wearing down **cliffs**.

• Atmospheric instability caused by the **greenhouse effect** and **global warming** appears to be increasing the severity of **Atlantic** storms and the heights of the ocean waves. Waves in the South Atlantic are shrinking – they are on average half a metre smaller than in the mid-1980s – and those in the northeast Atlantic have doubled in size over the last 40 years.

- As the height of waves affects the supply of marine food, this could affect fish stocks, and there are also implications for shipping and oil and gas rigs in the North Atlantic, which will need to be strengthened if they are to avoid damage.

Various schemes have been advanced for harnessing the energy of waves, but a major breakthrough will be required if wave power is ever to contribute significantly to the world's energy needs.

**See also**: *backwash, longshore drift.*

## weather
Day-to-day variation of atmospheric and climatic conditions at any one place over a short period of time. Weather conditions include **humidity**, **precipitation**, temperature, **cloud** cover, visibility, and **wind**, together with extreme phenomena such as **storms** and blizzards.

Weather forecasts are based on current meteorological data and predict likely weather for a particular area. They may be short-range (covering a period of one or two days), medium-range (five to seven days), or long-range (a month or so). Meteorologists, aided by communications and computer technology, are increasingly able to refine the accuracy of forecasts, but however sophisticated the techniques become there will always be an element of the unknown in any forecast which, as shown by **chaos theory**, is unlikely to be eliminated.

❝ Anyone can make a reasonable weather forecast, with 70% accuracy, just by predicting that tomorrow's weather will be the same as today's. ❞

**John Thorns**, of Birmingham University, on hearing of research into the accuracy of radio and television weather forecasters which found that the best of them had an accuracy rate of only 46%.
*Sunday Telegraph*, 29 November 1998

**See also**: *depression, front, meteorology, rain, wind.*

## weathering

Process by which exposed **rocks** are broken down by **rain, frost, wind**, and other elements of **weather**. Weathering differs from **erosion** because the broken down material is not transported. There are two main types of weathering, which usually occur together:

- *Physical weathering* includes such effects as freeze-thaw – the splitting of rocks by the alternate freezing and thawing of water trapped in cracks – and exfoliation, or onion-skin weathering, which is flaking caused by the alternate expansion and contraction of rocks in response to extreme changes in temperature.

- *Chemical weathering* involves a chemical change in the rocks affected, the most common form is caused by rainwater that has absorbed carbon dioxide from the atmosphere, forming a weak carbonic acid. This then reacts with certain **minerals** in the rocks and breaks them down. The formation of caverns in **limestone** terrain is an example.

A third type of weathering, *biological,* involves the disintegration of rocks brought about by the penetration of plant roots, and by the production of acids by those plants. Burrowing and grazing animals also contribute to this process.

**See also**: *inselberg.*

## Physical and chemical weathering

### physical weathering

| | |
|---|---|
| temperature changes | weakening rocks by expansion and contraction |
| frost | wedging rocks apart by the expansion of water on freezing |
| unloading | the loosening of rock layers by release of pressure after the erosion and removal of those layers above |

### chemical weathering

| | |
|---|---|
| carbonation | breakdown of calcite by reaction with carbonic acid in rainwater |
| hydrolysis | breakdown of feldspar into china clay by reaction with carbonic acid in rainwater |
| oxidation | breakdown of iron-rich minerals due to rusting |
| hydration | expansion of certain minerals due to the uptake of water |

## weir

Low dam built across a **river** to raise the level of the water and control its rate of flow.

### westerlies

Prevailing **winds** from the west which occur in both northern and southern hemispheres between latitudes of about 35° and 60°. They bring moist weather to the west coast of the landmasses in these areas. Unlike the **trade winds**, the westerlies are very variable and produce stormy weather.

### wetland

An area of land that is permanently wet, including **marshes**, fens, **bogs**, **flood plains**, and shallow coastal areas. Wetlands are extremely fertile. They provide warm, sheltered waters for fisheries, lush vegetation for grazing livestock, and an abundance of wildlife. Estuaries and seaweed beds are more than 16 times as productive in wetlands as in the open ocean.

The term wetland may also be applied to a naturally flooding area that is managed for agriculture or wildlife. A water meadow, where a river is expected to flood grazing land at least once a year thereby replenishing the soil, is a traditional example. Wetlands may also be managed to provide sanctuaries for wading birds and wild flowers.

### whirlwind

Rapidly rotating column of air, often called a **tornado**. On a smaller scale it produces the dust-devils seen in **deserts**.

### wilderness

Area of uninhabited land that has never been disturbed by humans, usually located some distance from towns and cities. According to estimates made in 1994, 52% (90 million sq km/35 million sq mi) of the Earth's total land area could be classified as wilderness.

### wind

The natural movements of the **atmosphere** relative to the surface of the **Earth**. Wind speed is measured using an anemometer or by using the **Beaufort scale**. Although modified by features such as land and water, there is a basic worldwide system of **trade winds**, **westerlies**, and **polar** easterlies. Local winds result from landmasses heating and cooling faster than the adjacent sea, producing onshore winds in the daytime and offshore winds at night. The fastest wind speed ever measured on Earth, 512 kph/318 mph, occurred on 3 May 1999 in a tornado that struck the suburbs of Oklahoma City, Oklahoma, USA. There are many types of wind.

- The **monsoon** is a seasonal wind of southern Asia, bringing the rain on which crops depend.
- Famous or notorious warm winds include the North American chinook, the föhn of Europe's Alpine valleys, and the sirocco (Italy).
- The dry northerly bise (Switzerland) and the mistral, which strikes the Mediterranean area of France, are unpleasantly cold winds.

## wind power
The harnessing of wind energy to produce power.

- After the energy crisis of the 1970s wind turbines began to be used to produce electricity on a large scale.
- In 1995 the UK generated nearly 350 megawatts from wind energy, a 10% increase from 1994.
- In October 1997 Denmark launched the first phase of its aim to generate 50% of its electricity requirements using wind by 2030, by announcing that 500 large turbines would be built off the coast by 2008. The country already has 4,000 smaller land turbines.

  **See also**: *energy, alternative; renewable resources.*

## world city
Cities widely recognized as centres of economic and political power within the capitalist world economy. The cities are important financial and business centres and usually boast a high concentration of headquarters of **multinational corporations**. London, New York, and Tokyo are world cities.

## xerophyte

Plant adapted to live in extremely dry conditions. Many **desert** cacti are xerophytes. In order to adapt, plants must reduce their rate of **transpiration**, by:

- growing small leaves, or sometimes just spines or scales
- having a dense covering of hairs over the leaf to trap a layer of moist air (as in edelweiss)
- developing water storage cells, sunken stomata, and permanently rolled leaves or leaves that roll up in dry weather (as in marram grass).

# Appendix

# World – physical

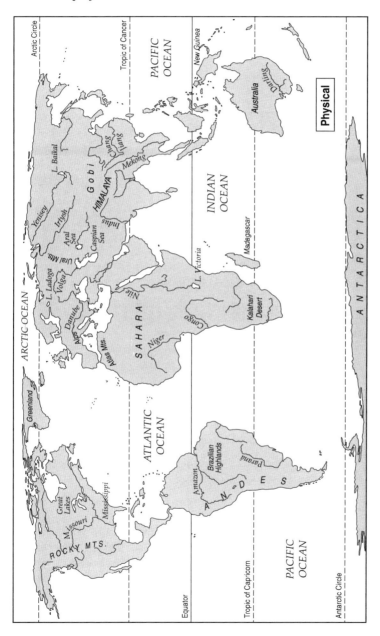

# World – climate regions

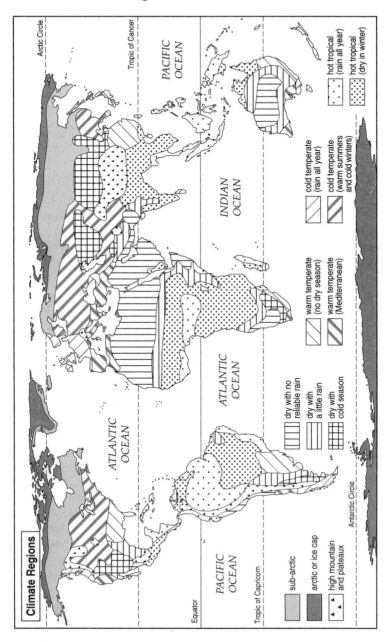

## Latitude, longitude, and altitude of the world's major cities

| City | Latitude | | Longitude | | Altitude | |
|---|---|---|---|---|---|---|
| | ° | ′ | ° | ′ | m | ft |
| Adelaide, Australia | 34 | 55 S | 138 | 36 E | 43 | 140 |
| Algiers, Algeria | 36 | 50 N | 03 | 00 E | 59 | 194 |
| Almaty, Kazakhstan | 43 | 16 N | 76 | 53 E | 775 | 2,543 |
| Amsterdam, Netherlands | 52 | 22 N | 04 | 53 E | 3 | 10 |
| Ankara, Turkey | 39 | 55 N | 32 | 55 E | 862 | 2,825 |
| Asunción, Paraguay | 25 | 15 S | 57 | 40 W | 139 | 456 |
| Athens, Greece | 37 | 58 N | 23 | 43 E | 92 | 300 |
| Bangkok, Thailand | 13 | 45 N | 100 | 31 E | 0 | 0 |
| Barcelona, Spain | 41 | 23 N | 02 | 09 E | 93 | 305 |
| Beijing, China | 39 | 56 N | 116 | 24 E | 183 | 600 |
| Belfast, Northern Ireland | 54 | 37 N | 05 | 56 W | 67 | 217 |
| Belgrade, Yugoslavia | 44 | 52 N | 20 | 32 E | 132 | 433 |
| Berlin, Germany | 52 | 31 N | 13 | 25 E | 34 | 110 |
| Bogotá, Colombia | 04 | 32 N | 74 | 05 W | 2,640 | 8,660 |
| Bombay, India | 18 | 58 N | 72 | 50 E | 8 | 27 |
| Brussels, Belgium | 50 | 52 N | 04 | 22 E | 100 | 328 |
| Bucharest, Romania | 44 | 25 N | 26 | 07 E | 92 | 302 |
| Budapest, Hungary | 47 | 30 N | 19 | 05 E | 139 | 456 |
| Buenos Aires, Argentina | 34 | 36 S | 58 | 28 W | 0 | 0 |
| Cairo, Egypt | 30 | 03 N | 31 | 15 E | 116 | 381 |
| Cape Town, South Africa | 33 | 55 S | 18 | 22 E | 17 | 56 |
| Caracas, Venezuela | 10 | 28 N | 67 | 02 W | 1,042 | 3,418 |
| Copenhagen, Denmark | 55 | 40 N | 12 | 34 E | 9 | 33 |
| Dakar, Senegal | 14 | 40 N | 17 | 28 W | 40 | 131 |
| Delhi, India | 28 | 35 N | 77 | 12 E | 218 | 714 |
| Detroit (MI), USA | 42 | 19 N | 83 | 02 W | 178 | 585 |
| Djibouti, Djibouti | 11 | 30 N | 43 | 03 E | 7 | 23 |
| Dublin, Republic of Ireland | 53 | 20 N | 06 | 15 W | 47 | 154 |
| Edinburgh, Scotland | 55 | 55 N | 03 | 10 W | 134 | 440 |
| Frankfurt, Germany | 50 | 07 N | 08 | 41 E | 103 | 338 |
| Guatemala City, Guatemala | 14 | 37 N | 90 | 31 W | 1,480 | 4,855 |
| Havana, Cuba | 23 | 08 N | 82 | 23 W | 24 | 80 |
| Helsinki, Finland | 60 | 10 N | 25 | 00 E | 46 | 151 |
| Hong Kong, China | 22 | 18 N | 114 | 10 E | 33 | 109 |

## Latitude, longitude, and altitude of the world's major cities (continued)

| City | Latitude | | Longitude | | Altitude | |
|---|---|---|---|---|---|---|
| | ° | ´ | ° | ´ | m | ft |
| Istanbul, Turkey | 41 | 06 N | 29 | 03 E | 114 | 374 |
| Jakarta, Indonesia | 06 | 10 S | 106 | 48 E | 8 | 26 |
| Jerusalem, Israel | 31 | 46 N | 35 | 14 E | 762 | 2,500 |
| Johannesburg, South Africa | 26 | 12 S | 28 | 05 E | 1,750 | 5,740 |
| Kabul, Afghanistan | 34 | 30 N | 69 | 13 E | 1,827 | 5,955 |
| Karachi, Pakistan | 24 | 48 N | 66 | 59 E | 4 | 13 |
| Katmandu, Nepal | 27 | 43 S | 85 | 19 E | 1,372 | 4,500 |
| Kiev, Ukraine | 50 | 26 N | 30 | 31 E | 179 | 587 |
| Kinshasa, Democratic Republic of Congo | 04 | 18 S | 15 | 17 E | 322 | 1,066 |
| Lagos, Nigeria | 06 | 27 N | 03 | 24 E | 3 | 10 |
| La Paz, Bolivia | 16 | 27 S | 68 | 22 W | 3,658 | 12,001 |
| Lhasa, Tibet | 29 | 40 N | 91 | 07 E | 3,685 | 12,090 |
| Lima, Peru | 12 | 00 S | 77 | 02 W | 120 | 394 |
| Lisbon, Portugal | 38 | 44 N | 09 | 09 W | 77 | 253 |
| London, UK | 51 | 32 N | 00 | 05 W | 75 | 245 |
| Los Angeles (CA), USA | 34 | 03 N | 118 | 14 W | 104 | 340 |
| Madrid, Spain | 40 | 26 N | 03 | 42 W | 660 | 2,165 |
| Manila, Philippines | 14 | 35 N | 120 | 57 E | 14 | 47 |
| Mecca, Saudi Arabia | 21 | 27 S | 39 | 49 E | 2,000 | 6,562 |
| Melbourne, Australia | 37 | 47 N | 144 | 58 E | 35 | 115 |
| Mexico City, Mexico | 19 | 24 N | 99 | 09 W | 2,239 | 7,347 |
| Milan, Italy | 45 | 27 S | 09 | 10 E | 121 | 397 |
| Montevideo, Uruguay | 34 | 53 N | 56 | 10 W | 22 | 72 |
| Moscow, Russia | 55 | 45 N | 37 | 35 E | 120 | 394 |
| Nagasaki, Japan | 32 | 48 S | 129 | 57 E | 133 | 436 |
| Nairobi, Kenya | 01 | 25 N | 36 | 55 E | 1,820 | 5,971 |
| New Delhi, India | 28 | 36 N | 77 | 12 E | 235 | 770 |
| New York (NY), USA | 40 | 45 N | 73 | 59 W | 17 | 55 |
| Oslo, Norway | 59 | 57 N | 10 | 42 E | 94 | 308 |
| Ottawa, Canada | 45 | 26 N | 75 | 41 W | 56 | 185 |
| Panamá, Panama | 08 | 58 N | 79 | 32 W | 0 | 0 |
| Paris, France | 48 | 52 N | 02 | 20 E | 92 | 300 |
| Prague, Czech Republic | 50 | 05 N | 14 | 26 E | 262 | 860 |

## Latitude, longitude, and altitude of the world's major cities (*continued*)

| City | Latitude | | Longitude | | Altitude | |
|---|---|---|---|---|---|---|
| | ° | ′ | ° | ′ | m | ft |
| Quito, Ecuador | 0 | 13 S | 78 | 30 W | 2,811 | 9,222 |
| Reykjavik, Iceland | 64 | 04 N | 21 | 58 W | 18 | 59 |
| Rio de Janeiro, Brazil | 22 | 43 S | 43 | 13 W | 9 | 30 |
| Rome, Italy | 41 | 53 N | 12 | 30 E | 29 | 95 |
| St Petersburg, Russia | 59 | 56 N | 30 | 18 E | 4 | 13 |
| Santiago, Chile | 33 | 27 S | 70 | 40 W | 1,500 | 4,921 |
| Seoul, South Korea | 37 | 34 N | 127 | 00 E | 10 | 34 |
| Shanghai, China | 31 | 10 N | 121 | 28 E | 7 | 23 |
| Singapore | 01 | 14 N | 103 | 55 E | 10 | 33 |
| Sofia, Bulgaria | 42 | 40 N | 23 | 20 E | 550 | 1,805 |
| Stockholm, Sweden | 59 | 17 N | 18 | 03 E | 44 | 144 |
| Sydney, Australia | 33 | 53 S | 151 | 12 E | 8 | 25 |
| Tehran, Iran | 35 | 40 N | 51 | 26 E | 1,110 | 3,937 |
| Tokyo, Japan | 35 | 42 N | 139 | 46 E | 9 | 30 |
| Toronto, Canada | 43 | 39 N | 79 | 23 W | 91 | 300 |
| Tripoli, Libya | 32 | 54 N | 13 | 11 E | 0 | 0 |
| Vancouver, Canada | 49 | 18 N | 123 | 04 W | 43 | 141 |
| Vienna, Austria | 48 | 14 N | 16 | 20 E | 203 | 666 |
| Warsaw, Poland | 52 | 15 N | 21 | 00 E | 110 | 360 |
| Washington, DC, USA | 38 | 53 N | 77 | 00 W | 8 | 25 |
| Wellington, New Zealand | 41 | 18 S | 174 | 47 E | 0 | 0 |
| Zurich, Switzerland | 47 | 21 N | 08 | 31 E | 493 | 1,618 |

## Longest rivers in the world

| River | Location | Approximate length | |
|---|---|---|---|
| | | km | mi |
| Nile | Africa | 6,695 | 4,160 |
| Amazon | South America | 6,570 | 4,083 |
| Chang Jiang (Yangtze) | China | 6,300 | 3,915 |
| Mississippi–Missouri–Red Rock | USA | 6,020 | 3,741 |
| Huang He (Yellow River) | China | 5,464 | 3,395 |
| Ob–Irtysh | China/Kazakhstan/Russia | 5,410 | 3,362 |
| Amur–Shilka | Asia | 4,416 | 2,744 |
| Lena | Russia | 4,400 | 2,734 |
| Congo–Zaire | Africa | 4,374 | 2,718 |
| Mackenzie–Peace–Finlay | Canada | 4,241 | 2,635 |
| Mekong | Asia | 4,180 | 2,597 |
| Niger | Africa | 4,100 | 2,548 |
| Yenisei | Russia | 4,100 | 2,548 |
| Paraná | Brazil | 3,943 | 2,450 |
| Mississippi | USA | 3,779 | 2,348 |
| Murray–Darling | Australia | 3,751 | 2,331 |
| Missouri | USA | 3,726 | 2,315 |
| Volga | Russia | 3,685 | 2,290 |
| Madeira | Brazil | 3,241 | 2,014 |
| Purus | Brazil | 3,211 | 1,995 |
| São Francisco | Brazil | 3,199 | 1,988 |
| Yukon | USA/Canada | 3,185 | 1,979 |
| Rio Grande | USA/Mexico | 3,058 | 1,900 |
| Indus | Tibet/Pakistan | 2,897 | 1,800 |
| Danube | central and eastern Europe | 2,858 | 1,776 |
| Japura | Brazil | 2,816 | 1,750 |
| Salween | Myanmar/China | 2,800 | 1,740 |
| Brahmaputra | Asia | 2,736 | 1,700 |
| Euphrates | Iraq | 2,736 | 1,700 |
| Tocantins | Brazil | 2,699 | 1,677 |
| Zambezi | Africa | 2,650 | 1,647 |
| Orinoco | Venezuela | 2,559 | 1,590 |
| Paraguay | Paraguay | 2,549 | 1,584 |
| Amu Darya | Tajikistan/Turkmenistan/Uzbekistan | 2,540 | 1,578 |
| Ural | Russia/Kazakhstan | 2,535 | 1,575 |
| Kolyma | Russia | 2,513 | 1,562 |
| Ganges | India/Bangladesh | 2,510 | 1,560 |
| Arkansas | USA | 2,344 | 1,459 |
| Colorado | USA | 2,333 | 1,450 |
| Dnieper | Russia/Belarus/Ukraine | 2,285 | 1,420 |
| Syr Darya | Asia | 2,205 | 1,370 |
| Irrawaddy | Myanmar | 2,152 | 1,337 |
| Orange | South Africa | 2,092 | 1,300 |

## Relative times in cities throughout the world*

| City | Time |
|---|---|
| Abu Dhabi, United Arab Emirates | 16:00 |
| Accra, Ghana | 12:00 |
| Addis Ababa, Ethiopia | 15:00 |
| Adelaide, Australia | 21:30 |
| Alexandria, Egypt | 14:00 |
| Algiers, Algeria | 13:00 |
| Al Manamah (also called Bahrain), Bahrain | 15:00 |
| Amman, Jordan | 14:00 |
| Amsterdam, Netherlands | 13:00 |
| Anchorage (AK), USA | 03:00 |
| Ankara, Turkey | 14:00 |
| Athens, Greece | 14:00 |
| Auckland, New Zealand | 24:00 |
| Baghdad, Iraq | 15:00 |
| Bahrain (also called Al Manamah), Bahrain | 15:00 |
| Bangkok, Thailand | 19:00 |
| Barcelona, Spain | 13:00 |
| Beijing, China | 20:00 |
| Beirut, Lebanon | 14:00 |
| Belgrade, Yugoslavia | 13:00 |
| Berlin, Germany | 13:00 |
| Bern, Switzerland | 13:00 |
| Bogotá, Colombia | 07:00 |
| Bombay, India | 17:30 |
| Bonn, Germany | 13:00 |
| Brazzaville, Republic of the Congo | 13:00 |
| Brisbane, Australia | 22:00 |
| Brussels, Belgium | 13:00 |
| Bucharest, Romania | 14:00 |
| Budapest, Hungary | 13:00 |
| Buenos Aires, Argentina | 09:00 |
| Cairo, Egypt | 14:00 |
| Calcutta, India | 17:30 |
| Canberra, Australia | 22:00 |
| Cape Town, South Africa | 14:00 |
| Caracas, Venezuela | 08:00 |

## Relative times in cities throughout the world* (*continued*)

| City | Time |
|------|------|
| Casablanca, Morocco | 12:00 |
| Chennai (formerly Madras), India | 17:30 |
| Chicago (IL), USA | 06:00 |
| Cologne, Germany | 13:00 |
| Colombo, Sri Lanka | 18:00 |
| Copenhagen, Denmark | 13:00 |
| Damascus, Syria | 14:00 |
| Dar es Salaam, Tanzania | 15:00 |
| Darwin, Australia | 21:30 |
| Delhi, India | 17:30 |
| Denver (CO), USA | 05:00 |
| Dhaka, Bangladesh | 18:00 |
| Dubai, United Arab Emirates | 16:00 |
| Dublin, Republic of Ireland | 12:00 |
| Florence, Italy | 13:00 |
| Frankfurt am Main, Germany | 13:00 |
| Gdańsk, Poland | 13:00 |
| Geneva, Switzerland | 13:00 |
| Gibraltar | 13:00 |
| Hague, The, Netherlands | 13:00 |
| Harare, Zimbabwe | 14:00 |
| Havana, Cuba | 07:00 |
| Helsinki, Finland | 14:00 |
| Hobart, Australia | 22:00 |
| Ho Chi Minh City, Vietnam | 19:00 |
| Hong Kong, China | 20:00 |
| Istanbul, Turkey | 14:00 |
| Jakarta, Indonesia | 19:00 |
| Jerusalem, Israel | 14:00 |
| Johannesburg, South Africa | 14:00 |
| Karachi, Pakistan | 17:00 |
| Kiev, Ukraine | 14:00 |
| Kuala Lumpur, Malaysia | 20:00 |
| Kuwait City, Kuwait | 15:00 |
| Kyoto, Japan | 21:00 |
| Lagos, Nigeria | 13:00 |
| Le Havre, France | 13:00 |

## Relative times in cities throughout the world* (*continued*)

| City | Time |
|------|------|
| Lima, Peru | 07:00 |
| Lisbon, Portugal | 12:00 |
| London, England | 12:00 |
| Luanda, Angola | 13:00 |
| Luxembourg, Luxembourg | 13:00 |
| Lyon, France | 13:00 |
| Madrid, Spain | 13:00 |
| Manila, Philippines | 20:00 |
| Marseille, France | 13:00 |
| Mecca, Saudi Arabia | 15:00 |
| Melbourne, Australia | 22:00 |
| Mexico City, Mexico | 06:00 |
| Milan, Italy | 13:00 |
| Minsk, Belarus | 14:00 |
| Monrovia, Liberia | 12:00 |
| Montevideo, Uruguay | 09:00 |
| Montreal, Canada | 07:00 |
| Moscow, Russian Federation | 15:00 |
| Munich, Germany | 13:00 |
| Nairobi, Kenya | 15:00 |
| New Orleans (LA), USA | 06:00 |
| New York (NY), USA | 07:00 |
| Nicosia, Cyprus | 14:00 |
| Oslo, Norway | 13:00 |
| Ottawa, Canada | 07:00 |
| Panamá, Panama | 07:00 |
| Paris, France | 13:00 |
| Perth, Australia | 20:00 |
| Port Said, Egypt | 14:00 |
| Prague, Czech Republic | 13:00 |
| Rawalpindi, Pakistan | 17:00 |
| Reykjavík, Iceland | 12:00 |
| Rio de Janeiro, Brazil | 09:00 |
| Riyadh, Saudi Arabia | 15:00 |
| Rome, Italy | 13:00 |
| San Francisco (CA), USA | 04:00 |
| Santiago, Chile | 08:00 |

## Relative times in cities throughout the world* (*continued*)

| City | Time |
|---|---|
| Seoul, South Korea | 21:00 |
| Shanghai, China | 20:00 |
| Singapore City, Singapore | 20:00 |
| Sofia, Bulgaria | 14:00 |
| St Petersburg, Russian Federation | 15:00 |
| Stockholm, Sweden | 13:00 |
| Sydney, Australia | 22:00 |
| Taipei, Taiwan | 20:00 |
| Tashkent, Uzbekistan | 17:00 |
| Tehran, Iran | 15:30 |
| Tel Aviv-Yafo, Israel | 14:00 |
| Tenerife, Canary Islands | 12:00 |
| Tokyo, Japan | 21:00 |
| Toronto, Canada | 07:00 |
| Tripoli, Libya | 13:00 |
| Tunis, Tunisia | 13:00 |
| Valparaiso, Chile | 08:00 |
| Vancouver, Canada | 04:00 |
| Vatican City | 13:00 |
| Venice, Italy | 13:00 |
| Vienna, Austria | 13:00 |
| Vladivostok, Russian Federation | 22:00 |
| Volgograd, Russian Federation | 16:00 |
| Warsaw, Poland | 13:00 |
| Wellington, New Zealand | 24:00 |
| Yangon (formerly Rangoon), Myanmar | 18:30 |
| Yokohama, Japan | 21:00 |
| Zagreb, Croatia | 13:00 |
| Zürich, Switzerland | 13:00 |

*At 12:00 noon, GMT.

The surface of the Earth is divided into 24 time zones. Each zone represents 15° of longitude or 1 hour of time. Countries to the east of London and the Greenwich meridian are ahead of Greenwich Mean Time (GMT) and countries to the west are behind. The time indicated in the table is fixed by law and is called standard time. Use of daylight saving time (such as British Summer Time) varies widely.